why do kids do that?

why do kids do that?

a practical guide to positive parenting skills

Dr Richard C. Woolfson

This edition published in 2005 for Index Books Ltd

First published in Great Britain in 2004 by
Hamlyn, a division of Octopus Publishing Group Ltd
2–4 Heron Quays, London E14 4JP

ISBN 0 600 61102 7

A CIP catalogue record for this book is available from the British Library

Printed and bound in China

contents

Introduction

You want the best for your child, you want other children and adults to like her, and you want her to get on well with her peers. Yet her behaviour doesn't happen by chance: the way your child interacts with others depends on a combination of different influences, including her personality, her abilities and talents, and the way she is brought up by you at home.

This book can help you as a parent to raise your child to become the wonderful person you want her to be. However, it is not a recipe book for success or a checklist of boxes to be ticked – rather, it is a guide to the theory and practice of child behaviour, to give you a better understanding of what makes your growing child tick and how you can support her.

Positive Parenting

There is no doubt that raising a child is demanding for much of the time. The minute you solve one problem, another emerges; the minute one crisis is over, another one arises. No wonder the pressures of managing your child's behaviour effectively get you down occasionally.

This book takes a positive approach to these very real problems, by encouraging you to look for solutions to the difficulties your child poses instead of focusing only on blame. It suggests techniques for preventing challenging behaviour, rather than concentrating purely on how to deal with difficult behaviour when it arises, and offers advice on building a strong, loving relationship with your child rather than dealing only with repairing the damage. This positive parenting approach will boost your self-confidence as a parent and develop your belief in your own effectiveness.

How This Book Works

This book deals with the common – and some less common – challenges facing today's parents, such as how to establish discipline at home with your growing child, the fair and

A happy, confident child will enjoy life's opportunities and cope with its challenges.

reasonable use of rewards and punishments, giving to your child without spoiling her, and teaching her self-control.

A wide range of other topics relevant to children from babyhood up to 8 years old are also covered, including eating habits and healthy diets, how to achieve stress-free bedtime routines, keeping your child busy and developing strong sibling relationships. Issues such as childhood fears and toddler tantrums are discussed, and strategies are suggested for developing the optimist in your child and helping her to make friends. Throughout, the book is packed with practical advice, top tips and information charts for quick and easy reference.

Loving parental support gives a child a great start as she learns to deal with the wider world.

Maintaining Perspective

As a parent, you need to be realistic. Do not expect too much of yourself or your child. Of course you have high expectations of your child's behaviour, but remember that although a great deal of childhood behaviour is challenging, it is normal, all the same.

For instance, toddler tantrums are common when your child is around 2 years old. At that age, unexpected explosions of temper are typical and they are extremely difficult to manage. Yet the fact that these episodes of rage are normal should reassure you that your child's behaviour is neither your fault not hers, but simply a combination of circumstances. Rather than allowing self-recrimination to flourish, it is better to look for positive solutions.

The same applies to many other aspects of child behaviour. Take shyness, for example. You may find that your 4-year-old chats excitedly about her best friend's party every single day in the weeks before it and is thrilled with the new dress you have bought her just for this occasion. She even takes delight in choosing her friend's birthday present. Yet the moment she arrives at her friend's house for the party itself she freezes, bursts out crying and refuses to cross the threshold. This sudden onset of shyness is challenging, but again it is normal. Fortunately, there is lots you can do to help your child overcome this temporary social hurdle.

This book will help you to understand your child's emotional, social and behavioural needs, enabling you to support her at all stages so that you do not expect too much. Suggested goals are realistic and attainable. This will allow you to keep a balanced perspective on parenting, irrespective of any pressures you may experience.

How to Use This Book

Use the book in a way that suits you. You could read it from cover to cover, or your attention could be drawn to specific chapters that are relevant to your child right now. Alternatively, you could use it as a reference book, depending on her stage of development. However you use this book, you and your child will benefit from your deeper understanding of her needs and how you can help her as she grows.

formative influences

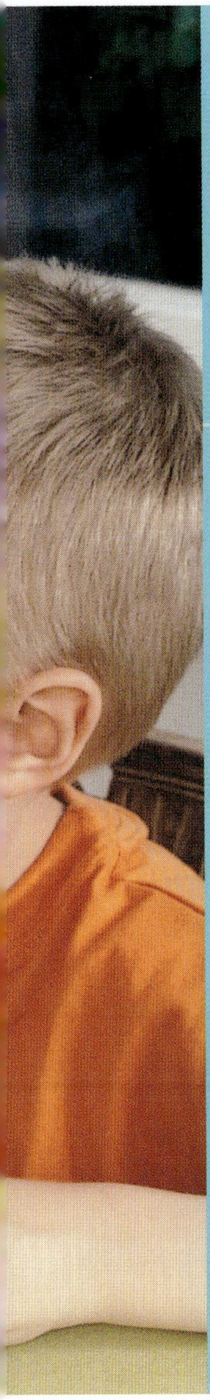

1 formative influences

- individual differences
- nature or nurture?
- personality types
- the family
- a sense of loss
- values and beliefs
- external influences
- parental influence
- parenting choices
- positive parenting
- an open mind
- be flexible
- cause for concern
- keeping a strong bond

Individual Differences

You need only glance at a group of children playing together to realize that they come in all sorts of shapes and sizes, with a wide range of abilities, skills and appearances. Each is wonderful in his own special way because he is unique, but he is not this way simply by chance. His genes – the inherited blueprints of physical and personal qualities that are passed from parent to child at the time of conception – play a huge part.

Conception

At the moment of conception, when a single sperm from the father penetrates the outer wall of the ovum (egg) inside the mother, two processes start to operate:

1. A biochemical reaction ensures all other sperm are rejected by the egg and it can only be fertilized by one sperm on one occasion.
2. The sperm and the egg both release their genetic material, which mixes and combines, resulting in the formation of a new cell. Called a 'zygote', this new cell – which scientists have shown is less than one-twentieth the size of a pinhead – contains all the blueprints for subsequent development.

5 Top Tips

1 Avoid confusing the physical and psychological dimensions.

Although there is clear evidence that most physical characteristics are inherited genetically, the evidence about personality is less clear.

2 Recognize the difference between potential and actual.

The fact that, say, your child could grow to a certain height does not mean that he will – this also depends on environmental support such as adequate food, good health care and balanced nutrition.

Physical characteristics like eye colour are determined by the combination of parental genes.

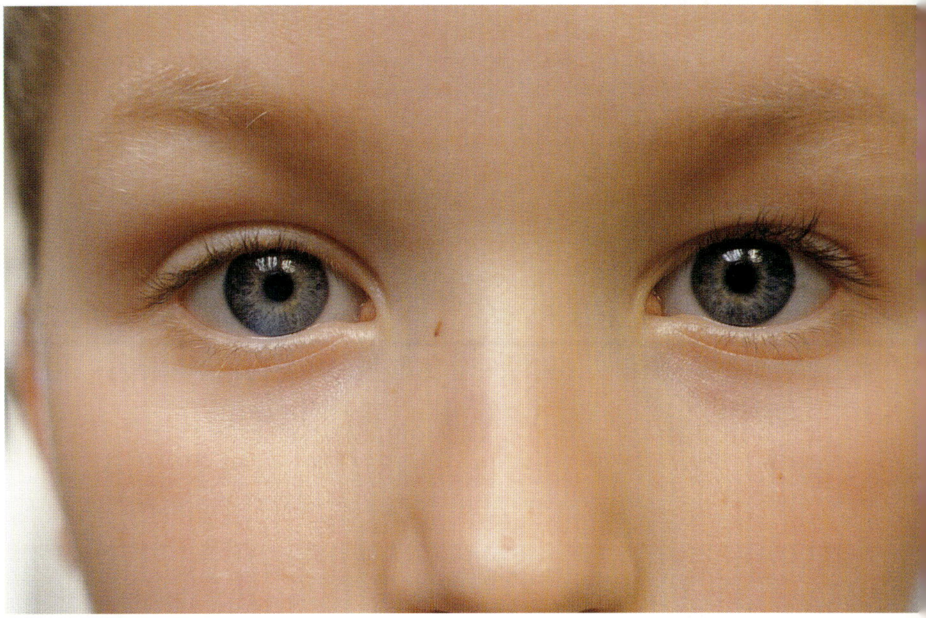

After conception, this single cell starts on its journey towards the uterus (womb), where it will remain until birth. However, as it moves along the zygote divides, then each of the divisions divide, and so on, until at the point of birth the baby is made up of literally billions of cells. This cell regeneration, called 'mitosis', continues throughout life – every new cell contains a replica of the genetic information contained in the original zygote.

Genes and Chromosomes

Each human cell typically contains 23 pairs of chromosomes, the parts of the cell that carry the growth blueprints. Two of these are sex chromosomes, while the rest are responsible for other characteristics. In male cells, one sex chromosome is type X and one is type Y, while in female cells both sex chromosomes are type X. Sperm cells have one sex cell, which can be X or Y, and the female egg cell's chromosome is always an X. So, at conception if the fertilizing sperm cell has an X chromosome, then a girl will be produced (XX). If the fertilizing sperm cell has a Y chromosome, then a boy will be produced (XY). Each of these chromosomes, which are present inside each cell, contains thousands of smaller particles, called 'genes'. These carry the instructions for physical development. They determine, for example, your child's size, the colour of his eyes, skin and hair, and his blood group.

From conception, each child's unique genetic inheritance make him an individual in looks and personality.

Dominant or Recessive

Genes interact in order to form complementary pairs. Some genes are dominant – their instructions will always have more authority – while other genes are recessive – their instructions have less authority than those of dominant genes and are only recognized by the body when both genes in the pair are recessive. For instance, the gene for brown eyes is dominant while the gene for blue eyes is recessive. At conception, if the gene pair has two 'brown' genes, or has one of each colour, the baby will have brown eyes (because the 'brown' gene always dominates over the 'blue' gene). Alternatively, if the gene pair has two 'blue' genes, the baby will have blue eyes (because there is no dominant 'brown' gene). That's why two brown-eyed parents can have a blue-eyed baby (when they both transmit a 'blue' gene to their child), but two blue-eyed parents cannot have a brown-eyed baby (because if either carried the 'brown' gene they would be brown-eyed themselves, as the 'brown' gene would dominate).

❸ Be proud of shared qualities.
You will probably be delighted when you see physical similarities between you and your child. (On the other hand, if you are disappointed that he has similarities to you, push these negative feelings to one side!)

❹ Be ready for individuality.
There will be some characteristics in your child that appear unrelated to either you or your partner – that's because genes can combine to form completely new traits.

❺ Consider genetic advice.
In instances where there is a family history of a particular gene-related health issue, you may be offered genetic counselling from medical staff in order to guide your family-planning decisions.

Nature or Nurture?

When you look at your growing child, you cannot help but wonder how she came to be the very distinctive individual she is, with her own special blend of personality, skills and talents. Of course, you are proud of the way she is turning out, yet it's only natural that you should be curious about the source of her individuality. You might be asking yourself 'Does she behave like this because of the way we have brought her up, or would she have behaved like this whoever her parents were?' This very basic question is what psychologists refer to as the nature/nurture debate.

In the past, professionals were split between two schools of thought:

1. Those who maintained that a child's personality and development are totally inborn, that the essential characteristics are present at birth and that the environment in which she grows up has little part to play.
2. Those who believed that a child is born as a 'blank slate', ready to have all aspects of her behaviour influenced and moulded by her environment. However, advances in research have now shown that these extreme views are almost certainly both inaccurate.

5 Top Tips

1 Have high expectations of your child's behaviour.

She doesn't always behave as you would like her to, but it is important that you have high expectations. This sets a standard for her.

2 Don't hide behind 'nature'.

When you are at a loss to understand some aspect of your child's behaviour, resist the temptation to tell yourself that you can do nothing about it.

Even a baby in the womb can be affected by its mother's emotions.

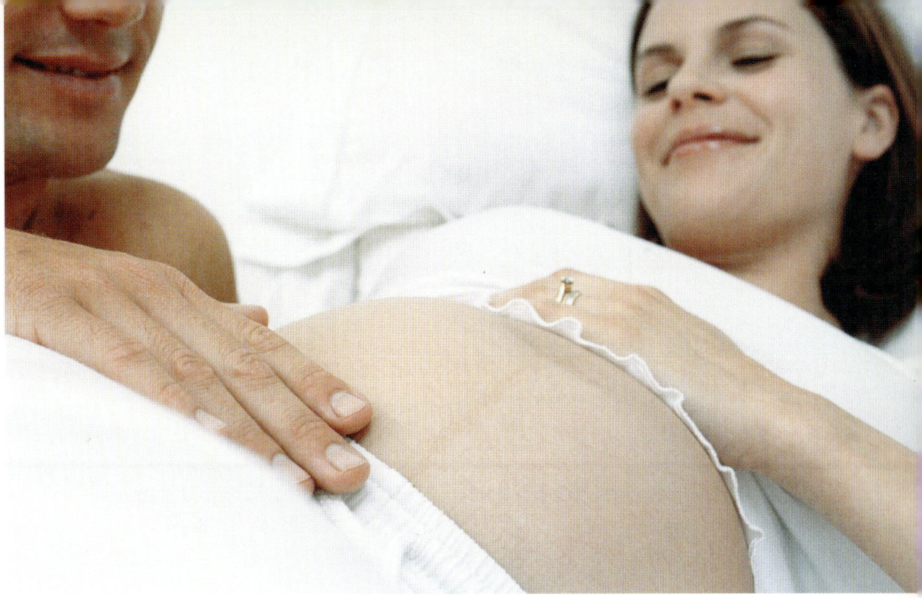

Interaction

Even before your baby is born, her experiences in the womb have an impact. For instance, scientists have shown that when the pregnant mother becomes agitated through stress, hormones are released spontaneously into her bloodstream – and these hormones cross the placenta, affecting the unborn baby, too. That's one reason why, for example, the heartbeat of a baby in the womb accelerates when the heartbeat of the pregnant mother accelerates. The mother's emotional state is connected to her unborn baby's emotional state.

Your baby arrives in the world with certain characteristics established. You only need to think about her when she was born. Maybe she behaved passively and lethargically, or perhaps she was active and restless. Maybe she took her first feed very slowly, or perhaps she gulped it down. Every baby behaves differently in those first hours, and this cannot be attributed to environmental influences. There is evidence that some psychological traits are inherited before the environment can have any effect.

You will see your child's personality start to emerge from the moment she is born.

However, there is also clear evidence that a child's upbringing has an impact on her behaviour. Common sense tells you this. For example, two children can have great determination to succeed. One might be encouraged to use that characteristic positively – for example, to reach high educational achievements. The other might use that characteristic negatively – for example, to get her own way every single time, no matter who else might be involved.

You also know from your everyday experience that your guidance can modify the way your child behaves in any situation. What you do to develop, encourage and nurture your child's behaviour influences the way she turns out to be. So, it is an interaction between 'nature' and 'nurture' that matters – neither aspect is sufficient on its own.

Parent and Child

The interaction is even more complicated than that, however, because *you* change, too, as a result of raising your child. You are not the same person as you were before you became a parent – you are different as a result of meshing your personality with that of your child as you bring her up. For instance, if your child is an anxious type you will have developed a gentle, subtle approach when introducing her to new experiences. Likewise, your child has changed to mesh with you. For example, if you are temperamental and easily upset, your child will be careful when asking you something. In other words, the way your child develops is a constant cycle of interaction between her inherent personality and the world around her, each of them impacting upon and changing the other.

❸ Look for gradual changes.

Whether your child's behaviour is inherited or acquired through interaction, change takes time. It makes sense to look for progress in small, gradual steps forward.

❹ Take a positive approach.

Every one of her personality traits – even those that prove to be challenging – can be used positively if you guide and support her appropriately.

❺ Value your child.

You will have more impact on the development of your growing child's behaviour when she feels that you value her for who she is, not simply for what she achieves.

Personality Types

Psychological research has shown that children's birth order has an effect on their behaviour. There is a 'typical' personality associated with a first-born child, which is different from the 'typical' personality associated with a second-born child, and so on. A first-born child is usually serious-minded, high achieving and more anxious; a second-born child tends to be unconventional, creative rather than logical, and have an inclination towards risk-taking; youngest children are often resourceful and self-confident, ready to make decisions on their own.

First-Born Child

As the first in the family, your child has your undivided love, attention and resources, probably for a couple of years. Small wonder, then, that a first-born child often achieves more educationally than his siblings – the child-centred interest, time and stimulation that come from his parents in the early years probably give him this head start. However, he also experiences responsibility and pressures because his parents probably push him harder, which may be why he tends to be more anxious than his later-born siblings.

Personality differences between siblings may be partly due to their relative positions in the family.

5 Top Tips

❶ Treat each of your children as a unique individual.

Whatever his birth order within the family, your child needs to know that he is special to you and just as important as his siblings.

❷ Recognize and develop talents.

You may have particular aspirations for your child but he has hopes, too. Allow him to develop his own aims, rather than forcing him into a role.

Support and encourage your children's talents or interests.

What You Can Do

- Let your first-born develop his own interests and skills.
- Do not pressurize him to achieve at school in order to fulfil your own dreams and aspirations.
- Encourage a broad range of activities, not just those connected with formal schooling.
- Let him know that everybody makes mistakes sometimes and has occasional failures.

Subsequent Children

Having an older brother or sister around when he arrives in the world means that your child gets used to sharing from the moment he is born (assuming the age gap is not so great that the older sibling is entirely independent). Psychologists believe that this child's liking for the unconventional could stem from the fact that his older sibling is so scholarly – the later-born child opts for an alternative lifestyle rather than having to compete. However, it is also possible that the younger child picks up a lot of information from his older brother or sister and may therefore appear older than his years. He prefers creative activities, as these allow him to express his individuality, and is more likely to challenge parental rules.

What You Can Do

- Avoid using your first-born child's achievements as a goal for your next child – this could actually de-motivate him. He wants to grow as an individual in his own right rather than follow in the footsteps of an older sibling.
- Encourage the creative side of his personality.
- Stick to your family rules despite his objections.

Youngest Child

Irrespective of how many older siblings he has, your youngest child is likely to be confident and independent. The most likely explanation for this is that he has had to fight for his share of the family's resources right from the start. He is often at the end of the queue when it comes to new clothes, choosing games or making a contribution to family discussions, and therefore learns to manage on his own. Nevertheless, guidance from his older siblings provides him with a sense of security and emotional safety.

What You Can Do

- Remember that your youngest child has as many aspirations and feelings as your older children.
- He gets fed up having to wait his turn to have his say, so let him be first in the queue sometimes.
- Treat him seriously and listen to what he has to say.
- Make sure your other children do not dismiss his ideas simply because he is the youngest.

❸ Distribute resources fairly.

There is no reason why your first-born should always be the one who chooses on behalf of all your children. The others can have their turn at being first to choose, too.

❹ Do your best to avoid comparisons.

Your children can love each other without having to be like each other. Comparisons between siblings are usually divisive with negative results.

❺ Be aware of birth-order effects.

Now that you know there are specific psychological pressures associated with birth order, take steps to ensure that these pressures are managed effectively.

The Family

The structure of the typical nuclear family – that is, parents and their children – is far more varied today than in previous decades. While for many the nuclear family still consists of two married parents with two or three children all living together under one roof, changes in modern society mean that there are now many variations on this model.

For instance, families may:

- Be headed by a single parent (either mother or father).
- Consist of a biological parent and a step-parent, plus children of one or both.
- Include large age gaps between the children.
- Be headed by parents who live in separate cities for much of the week due to work demands.

Whatever your particular family structure, your child needs you as much as the previous generation's children needed their parents. Increasing social complexity means that a child's world is increasingly complex, too. However, her basic emotional need to be loved, valued, encouraged and stimulated remains constant. Responsibility for bringing up your child and for guiding her behaviour still rests with you irrespective of your family structure, or job situation.

Home life remains the key psychological resource for your child's development. It is through positive family relationships that she starts to build her self-esteem, identity, self-belief and goals for life. She relies on you for love, guidance, support and encouragement. The

Grandparents may be able to offer valuable one-to-one attention at times when parents are busy.

5 Top Tips

❶ Encourage visits to your extended family.

You might like to rest and relax at weekends rather than visit your family members, but it is in your child's best interests to have at least occasional contact with these relatives.

❷ Respect grandparents.

There is no doubt that grandparents can have strong views, which you may feel undermine your authority as a parent. However, you should still let your child see that you respect them.

Positive relationships with other family members provide a vital support structure for a child.

nuclear family – in every format – is a context in which your child should be able to thrive.

The Extended Family

Members of your extended family also have a huge role to play in your child's life. Let's start with the other children, such as nephews and nieces. Your child learns important social skills from mixing with her cousins; she also takes on board new ideas and experiences fresh opportunities. Cousins are very special for a young child, even when she only sees them occasionally at family gatherings.

Then there are your child's aunts and uncles. In many extended families, a close emotional bond forms between aunts and uncles and their nephews and nieces. For example, sometimes a child is prepared to accept advice from an uncle even though she has previously rejected the same comments from her father. This happens because of the different nature of relationships within extended and nuclear families. Each of these relationships has a special part to play in your children's lives.

Finally, there are grandparents. Children almost always form a special connection with their grandparents, who are typically more patient and indulgent and have more spare time to devote to their grandchildren. Grandparents are also often used as a handy babysitting resource! Of course, grandparents (and other members of the extended family) can be a source of annoyance at times and may even have different views regarding the way children should be raised, which they may be quite happy to express – totally unsolicited. Nevertheless, they can be a very important part of a child's life, all through childhood and even into adulthood.

Grandparents also give your child a sense of continuity, tradition and family history. They can talk to her about the time when you were a child yourself. This is a rich source of pleasure and information for your growing child, and helps to strengthen the bond that exists between the generations.

❸ Resolve disagreements.

Try to resolve arguments with members of your extended family as swiftly as possible. Your child will be upset and disadvantaged by long-term ill-feeling in your family.

❹ Value your own role.

Remind yourself that the role played by your nuclear family in your child's life remains central to her growth and development, despite any changes in wider society.

❺ Have regular family get-togethers.

The hard work required to arrange these family occasions is almost always worthwhile, as they reinforce family bonds and confirm the role of traditions in your child's life.

A Sense of Loss

Disruption to family life that results in your child losing ready access to one of his parents – either through separation, divorce or bereavement – can have a devastating psychological impact on his development. Although every child is different, each with his own strengths and weaknesses, the loss of a parent will turn his world upside down. That's why he needs your sensitive support during those difficult times.

Divorce

The chances are that your child likes his family the way it is right now (as long as stresses at home are not too severe). Of course, he moans and groans and gets angry with you and your partner now and again. Yet family life with both of you is his rock. Separation and divorce takes this security from him, so it is hardly surprising that he may react adversely to the realization that the emotional world he knows at home is about to change. In some instances, a child's home changes, too, if the divorce involves a shift in finances and spending power.

Research has consistently shown that, in most instances, the children who emerge emotionally intact from parental separation or divorce are the ones who keep regular contact with both parents. Almost certainly your child still loves both of you, no matter what went on between you leading up to the split itself.

What You Can Do

Your child does not want to choose one parent over the other, so do not put him in that situation. Whatever the arguments between you and your ex-partner, sort them out when your child is not there. Do not drag him into your disputes, as this will

During a family break-up a child needs both parents to give him emotional stability and reassurance.

5 Top Tips

❶ Treat your child's feelings seriously.

Although your own sense of loss preoccupies you, your child's feelings are very significant. His emotions matter as much as yours.

❷ Give explanations.

Tell your child what is happening – do not keep him in the dark. Pitch your explanations at a level he can understand, using age-appropriate terms and language.

Changes in behaviour, like becoming withdrawn, can be a sign that your child is under stress.

make him feel worse. Whatever you do, do not let him feel responsible. Many children feel guilty and there are often divided loyalties.

Things may appear bleak, but you can rebuild a home life. You will work hard with your child, and you and your ex-partner must put your child's interests ahead of your own. He needs stability rather than chaos, calmness not bitterness – and, most important, easy access to both parents wherever possible (unless he may be at risk physically). Remember, too, that both parents should try to provide consistency in parenting style.

Bereavement

Given that even adults struggle with the concept of death, you can reasonably expect your child to have difficulty understanding what it means. You might find, for instance, that you carefully explain to him that his grandmother has died, and then he immediately asks if he can visit her as usual. Like you, he needs time to adjust to the idea of death and bereavement.

Studies have found that even toddlers can go through a genuine grief reaction. In other words, your child feels the same emotional pain that adults go through and therefore needs the same support during this very demanding period in his life. The problem is that adults are often so engrossed by their own grief that they pay little attention to the upset a child could be experiencing at the same time.

What You Can Do

Watch for changes in your child's behaviour that could indicate he is stressed. Apart from the obvious tears, look out for sleeplessness, bedwetting, irritability, loss of appetite, increased bickering with friends and withdrawal. Any or all of these (and other) alterations from his usual behaviour could indicate a grief reaction. During this period, your child requires extra attention and reassurance.

❸ Be honest.

Whether you are experiencing separation, divorce or bereavement, give your child honest answers to his questions. If you mislead him at this stage, you will only have to tell him the truth later. However, be careful not to give inappropriate details.

❹ Let your child speak.

He needs the opportunity to voice his feelings. Sometimes you may be uncomfortable with what he says to you, but he should be allowed to say it anyway, even if that includes some implied criticisms of you.

❺ Look to the future.

No matter how bleak you and your child may feel at present, the emotional pain will pass. By supporting each other now, your sense of loss will ease in time.

Values and Beliefs

Although you are the greatest single influence on the development of your child's behaviour, wider social contexts, like culture and religion, also play a part in your child's life – directly (by affecting his thoughts and ideas) and indirectly (by affecting your thoughts and ideas, which in turn affect his). By understanding the prevailing cultural and religious values in your child's life, you will be able to understand him better.

Cultural influences not linked to parental beliefs and attitudes include ethnic background. Each ethnic group has its own distinctive belief system, which plays a part in directing a child's behaviour.

Cultural Values

The culture in which your child is raised can be defined as the values, attitudes and beliefs of the main figures in his life. For example, you may believe strongly in the concept of respect for others or that physical violence between children is not to be tolerated. Your child absorbs this and builds his own view of the world which reflects these values.

A child can experience difficulties adjusting when the cultural values of his home life – whether derived from his parents' own beliefs or from a wider system of cultural beliefs related to ethnic background – do not match the values of the world in which he mixes. For instance, a child who has been raised to resolve conflict through discussion rather than violence will face an uphill struggle if confronted by children with the opposite attitude. Your challenge is to help your child mix in a world outside the home while still retaining your family's core cultural values, which is not always easy to achieve.

Stimulate him with information suited to his age and interests.

5 Top Tips

❶ Teach your child about his cultural history.

He benefits from understanding his past. This enables him to understand his origins and provides him with a direction for the future.

❷ Explain religious rituals.

As well as getting your child involved in the rituals associated with your religion, explain their underlying meaning to him so that he has good understanding.

Teaching your children about other religions and cultures helps them relate to the world around them.

Religion

Children are very trusting by nature and they generally warm to the concept of an all-caring deity who looks after them at all times. Young children frequently express religious beliefs – taught to them by their parents – with full conviction; and doubts are unusual in young children. That's why your religious beliefs are easily transmitted to your child, whether you are committed to a specific faith or are an atheist or an agnostic.

If religion plays a part in your life, your child will be particularly fascinated and engaged by its rituals of associated artefacts. For instance, he will look forward to regular visits to your place of worship and the rituals connected to your religion's festivals, especially if these events are shared with other members of your extended family.

Even if you have some doubts about the basis of religion, your child will take delight in sharing these sorts of events with you. An interest in religion that starts in the early years of childhood can lay the foundation for a lifelong commitment.

Be Aware

It is important to be aware of cultural dimensions in your child's life. Think about yourself for a moment. Write down three beliefs you hold about the right way to raise children. You might, for example, write 'a child should be loved', 'a child should never be smacked' and 'a child should be quietly spoken when with adults'. You may be surprised to discover how closely your child's behaviour is linked to these.

❸ Give him confidence in his culture.

Prepare him for some of the challenges to his values that he might experience when mixing with other children. Encourage him to have pride in what he believes.

❹ Broaden his mind.

It's not enough to accept and value his own culture – your child should also appreciate the cultures of other people. Try to broaden his outlook through discussion and explanation.

❺ Praise him for sticking to his cultural attitudes.

Let him know you are delighted that he stuck to his beliefs when other children urged him to behave differently. That takes courage.

External Influences

In addition to the values and beliefs of your family, your child is influenced by external factors, such as television programmes and his peer group. It is difficult to ensure that their effect on your child does not clash with your own ideas. You cannot be with him all the time, and he will learn to make his own decisions anyway, but you can guide him, giving him strategies for managing external pressures that could affect his behaviour.

Television

Under certain conditions, television is good for your child. In principle, there is nothing to be afraid of in allowing him to watch it during the day or in the evening. Television can add an exciting dimension to his life by letting him see places he has not yet visited, presenting him with new ideas and images, and helping to develop his interests. Programmes for children are more likely to be of good quality, with relevant and appropriate content, so using television programmes as part of an overall daily regime of stimulation can be positive.

Top Tips 5

❶ Do not leave unsuitable videos and DVDs lying around your house.

Your pre-school child is technologically competent – he can watch videos and DVDs without your help.

❷ Advise him about behaviour outside the family home.

Speak to him before he plays with other children. Be sensitive to social pressures, and encourage him to follow what he knows already.

Difficulties can arise, however, when your child watches programmes created for an older audience. This can be a legitimate cause for parental concern. There is usually nothing to be gained – and plenty to be lost – from a young child watching an adult-oriented programme. In this situation, the television becomes a developmental liability rather than an asset.

It may be wise to monitor computer games to make sure they are appropriate for your child's age.

When planning your child's viewing, an effective technique is to ensure that he watches a broad range of programmes, not just the same type over and over again. This means that the negative effects of any one particular programme can be offset by the positive effects of all the others. That's why you should have active involvement in structuring his television viewing behaviour. By all means, let him watch his favourite video time and again (assuming the content is appropriate), but encourage diversity in viewing, too.

Television is entertaining but social contact, reading and exercise should be part of a child's relaxation too.

Other Children

The older your child gets, the more he mixes with other children – and the more he is affected by their attitudes and behaviour. That's when he starts to justify his actions by saying 'All my friends do this.' These pressures begin from the moment he has pre-school contact with his peers. It can be frightening to realize how susceptible your child is to social pressures to conform.

What You Can Do

Rather than growing annoyed with him for so easily following the crowd, try to help your child to resist these social pressures so that he can stand on his own two feet and make his own decisions. The best way to do this is by giving him explanations for your family rules and values from an early age.

If he understands why, for example, it is wrong to take a toy from another child without asking (because it will upset them, because he wouldn't like that to happen to him, and so on), then he is more likely to resist the temptation to do this even when goaded to do so by others. If he has no idea why you have certain rules, his resistance to breaking them when he is with his friends will be weak.

❸ Decide on the amount of television time you will allow.

It's always useful to set limits on the amount of time for which your child sits in front of the screen each day. This also helps him to plan his activities.

❹ Discuss television programmes with your child.

Once a programme is over, talk to him about its content. Ask him to explain his thoughts about the programme. This develops his critical thinking.

❺ Don't blame the victim.

Of course, there will be times when he succumbs to external influences – that's only natural. Instead of blaming him, however, explain why his behaviour was unacceptable and give him strategies for thinking independently.

Parental Influence

By the time you have read about the roles of genetics, birth order, your nuclear and extended families, society, your culture and religion, and even television and other external influences, you might be left wondering if mum and dad make a difference at all! Do not be in any doubt – your role in raising your child and guiding her behaviour can override any of these other factors. What you do counts more than anything else.

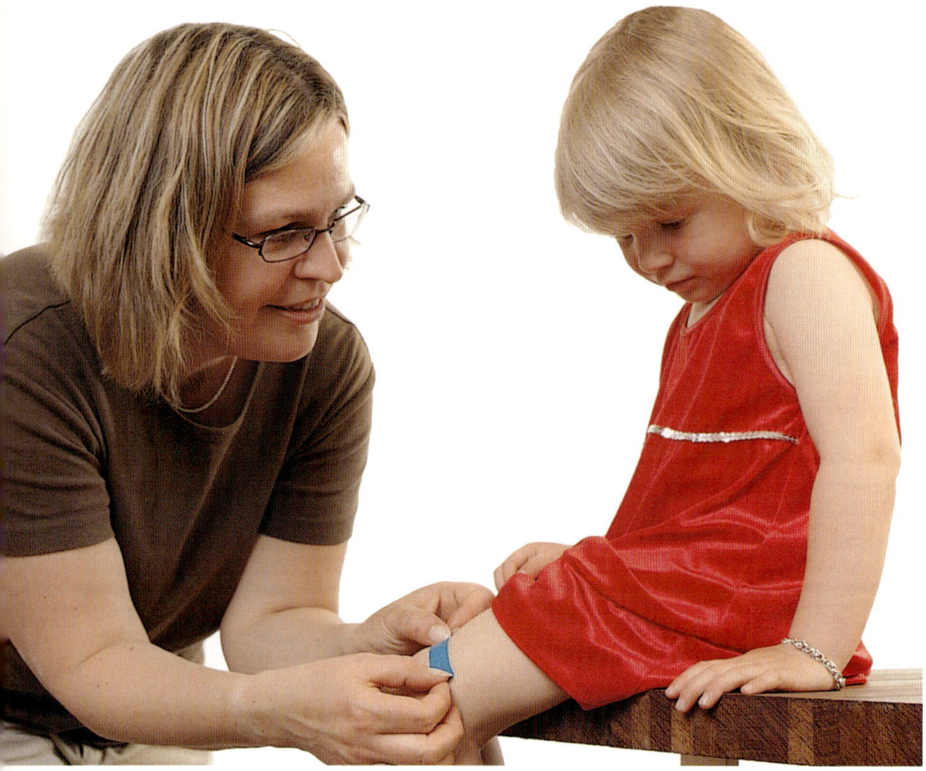

There are times when you see your child behave in a disappointing way, because it runs counter to your values and standards, and contrasts with the way you have encouraged her to behave. This can create a parental mind set in which you feel powerless, leading to the belief that in the end your child will behave in certain ways irrespective of the views you hold and guidance you give. Resist the temptation to take such a passive approach.

Spoiling

A spoilt child is generally unpopular with her peers and not very well liked by the adults in her world. Her self-centred demands and her expectations that everything should revolve around her create barriers between herself and other people. However, no child is born spoilt – it is not an inherited characteristic. Spoiling is something that parents and grandparents do to a child because it makes them feel good. If you think your child is spoiled, do something about it instead of simply accepting the situation passively. This is an area in which you can easily make a difference.

What You Can Do

In order to bring about change, you need to gain a better understanding of your own motivation.

Your influence as a parent is central to your child's development.

5 Top Tips

❶ Accept responsibility.

Tell yourself that you can influence all aspects of your child's behaviour, no matter what else goes on in her life at the same time. Your impact is paramount.

❷ Set realistic targets.

Don't expect too much, too soon. If you want to change your child's behaviour in some way, aim to achieve steady, gradual change.

To start with, think about all the possible reasons why your child has become spoilt:

- Have you allowed your child's grandparents to over-indulge her?
- Are you a working parent who over-compensates by being over-indulgent at home and avoiding conflict?
- Did you have what you now feel was a deprived childhood yourself and therefore shower your own child with presents and freedom so that her childhood is different?

If you locate the root of spoiling in your child's grandparents – because they let her do what she wants – speak to them about this, not to your child. Explain the difficulties you feel this is causing; emphasize that you know they do this out of love, but also point out the problems it causes when she mixes with other people.

If you are responsible for spoiling, do something about it. Be prepared to set limits and to say 'no' – remind yourself that in the long run, spoiling is not in your child's best interests.

Over-Protection

The same applies here. A child's increased nervousness about her physical safety and fear of new experiences can stem from parental management. Quite rightly, you place safety high on the agenda and do everything you can to keep your child from danger. However, you have to draw a line between encouraging sensible behaviour and being so over-protective that you make her afraid. Your approach to this issue makes a big difference.

What You Can Do

It is far better to teach your growing child how to look after herself than to keep her at home for as long as you can. She has to learn to look after herself at some point and she cannot achieve this without having experience of making decisions about safety for herself.

Letting your child explore by herself will help her grow in confidence and learn how to keep herself safe.

❸ Be self-critical.

Be prepared to ask yourself, 'Is there anything I can do differently so that my child does not behave in this way?' Her behaviour is inextricably linked to you.

❹ Have self-awareness.

Think about the motivations underlying your parenting behaviour. This will help you to understand why you set your family rules and why you have these expectations of your child.

❺ Work together in partnership with your child.

She needs your support and guidance so that she can gain confidence in making judgements about behaviour when you are not with her.

Parenting Choices

Parenting is one of the most important responsibilities you can ever have and yet so many people drift into it without giving any serious thought to the type of parent they want to be. That's a pity, because it's not just a matter of luck that you have become the sort of parent you are. Whether consciously or subconsciously, you determine the way you behave as a parent and decide on the family rules you establish at home.

The choices you make as a parent are influenced by your experiences, including your upbringing, the attitudes and values transmitted to you by your parents and specific memories from your childhood. You are also influenced by contemporary sources such as current social trends and the media. In the end, however, you have the choice to become the parent you want to be, so think carefully about this.

Parenting Styles

The first priority is for you to decide how you intend to encourage your child's development:

- **Some parents believe in rule-based parenting** in which behavioural rules are set out clearly very early on in life and the child is expected to conform to them at all times. These parents firmly believe that this is the best way to raise a balanced, well-adjusted child.
- **Other parents believe in a more nurturing style of parenting** in which love, trust and relationships are seen as more important than blind obedience to behavioural rules.

You'll pick a style that best suits your own personality and values.

Whatever type of parent you are, if you enjoy the time you spend with your child she will enjoy it too.

5 Top Tips

❶ Be active, not passive.
Instead of casually slipping into a parenting style, make positive choices from the start. However, be ready for flexibility when the need arises.

❷ Justify your choices.
Explain to yourself why you have chosen to be a particular type of parent. There should be good reasons for your choice, and these should be child-centred.

The next step is to sort out your goals for your child; these influence your parenting style. Most children need a mix of goals. For example:

- **If you think academic achievement is the prime goal in life** you will focus much of your time and attention on educational activities with your child. You will invest heavily in early learning experiences and toys that further her learning and understanding of concepts.
- **If you think social skills are of primary importance in life** you will concentrate more on how to help your growing child mix comfortably with others her own age.

Ups and Downs

The fact that you want to become a certain type of parent does not mean you will automatically achieve this. There is nothing wrong in having aspirations even though you do not always reach them. It is far better for you to aim to be a particular type of parent than to wander aimlessly through the experience without any clear sense of direction or purpose.

At times you will manage your child in exactly the way you envisaged – and you'll be delighted with yourself. At other times, you'll wish you had handled the situation differently – your confidence as a parent drops as a result. This is perfectly normal. Parenting will always be a series of mini-successes and mini-failures.

It is human nature to compare yourself with other people, as you judge your performance as a parent against their actions. However, do not always assume that they are better parents than you, just because they do things differently with their child. Watch other parents, learn from them if there is an opportunity, but try to retain the positive aspects of your own individuality – after all, that's one of the reasons why your child loves you so much.

If you want your child to help out at home let her start assisting you from an early age when she will think it is great fun.

❸ Put your child first.

You matter, too, as well as your child, but your job is to look out for her. Parenting is most effective when based on your child's needs, not yours.

❹ Check it out.

The best way to judge if your type of parenting suits your child is her happiness, well-being and general developmental progress. If she is miserable, think again.

❺ Implement change, not guilt.

Only the very lucky few get parenting absolutely right from the very beginning – almost all of us learn through our mistakes. Reject guilt and consider change instead.

Positive Parenting

No matter how much you love your child, parenting will feel overwhelming at times. There is always so much to be done, so many child-related problems to be solved, so many demands made on you that it is not surprising that parenting can seem like a juggling act in which your emotions, resources and energy are constantly being challenged.

The situation can be even more extreme when your child is young, because you spend a lot more time in her company at that stage. The best way to keep your swinging emotions under control is through the technique known as 'positive parenting', which encourages you to adopt a positive outlook.

Positive Steps

Positive parenting is not based on pretence. In other words, you do not have to kid yourself that you are happy with life as a parent when in reality you are totally run down, demotivated and exhausted. Pretence is not part of positive parenting. Rather, it involves focusing on the good points and becoming an active participant who makes positive decisions as a parent.

- **Detach yourself from your daily routine.** Reflect on the structure of the regular schedule you have with your child. Decide on the most demanding parts of the day and ask yourself if these can be arranged in other ways – to take place at other times of the day when you are less tired maybe, or perhaps they can be left out altogether. For example, your infant won't suffer

Ignore routine tasks occasionally and take time to share quiet moments reading or looking at photos together.

5 Top Tips

❶ **Make routine activities fun.**
Turn essential tasks – for instance, feeding or changing – into a game by making a special effort to sing or chat to your child while they are going on. These are also good learning experiences for her.

❷ **Recognize your achievements.**
The fact that you have spent the day caring for your demanding baby is proof of your abilities. Be pleased that you looked after her today.

If you need some time to yourself, call on a friend or relative to look after your child for a few hours.

irrevocable damage by missing out on her bath for one day. Rearranging your routine activities could significantly reduce your feelings of tiredness.

- **Actively develop confidence in yourself as a parent.** You are doing a job, even though things go wrong sometimes. Nobody gets parenting right all the time. Recognize and be proud of your strengths, instead of bemoaning your perceived failings as a parent. Too much time spent concentrating on what goes wrong dulls your appreciation of what works well for you and your child.
- **Value your child's progress and achievements.** During the pre-school years she changes in lots of different ways – there is a good chance that her development moves forward in some way every single day, whether she is more agile, uses more words or manages to solve the jigsaw puzzle that proved so difficult yesterday. This is part of the delight of being a parent, so make sure that these wonderful progressions are prominent in your mind, pushing the more difficult moments you have with her into second place. Be sure to let her know that you are pleased with her progress – your child's pleasure at your reaction reinforces your own positive feeling, making the experience more pleasurable for you both.
- **Remember that parenting need not be a one-person job.** Whether or not you have a partner – and if you do, your partner should play a role in sharing parenting tasks – your family and friends can come to your rescue when it all gets a bit much. A helping hand from a grandparent, brother or sister, or from a friend lifts the load from you for a while. A few hours' away from parenting gives you a chance to rest and build up your motivation once more.

❸ Keep criticism in perspective.

Your self-confidence may be weakened by criticism from someone else, but remember that this is only their opinion. However, if you think the comments are valid, take them on board and do something about them!

❹ Use babysitters effectively.

You will benefit from a change in routine. Organizing babysitters can be difficult, but you will feel better after this change to your typical day.

❺ Look at mementoes.

Looking through reminders of your child's early life, such as old baby clothes or family photographs, can quickly put you in a cheerier mood because they remind you of happy moments and earlier achievements.

An Open Mind

You will already have discovered that everybody has their own views on the way a child should be raised – and they are each convinced that theirs is absolutely right! By all means develop a strong sense of self-belief, but bear in mind that you have to work with others when raising your child – partner, nanny, childminder or nursery staff. Parenting rarely functions in isolation.

Consistency

No matter how few or how many adults are playing their part in caring for your child, they must all pull together in order that your child is managed consistently.

Inconsistent parenting – in which one parent works to one set of rules while the other works to a different set – is guaranteed to confuse your child. He won't know who to please first, or which standards he should follow. Worse still, he might play one parent off against the other with that time-worn phrase 'But mum/dad says I can do this.' Consistency provides a structure for your child: he knows how he is expected to behave. On the other hand, inconsistency frequently results in unhappiness for both child and parents.

This applies to all carers, not just to your partner. You should collaborate with your childminder, so that your child does not have to adjust to different standards depending on who is looking after him at a particular time. Chat to your child's carers about this, making sure that you all have a similar understanding when it comes to the way he is expected to

Show your interest in how your child and her carer have spent their day by taking a moment to chat at pick-up time.

5 Top Tips

❶ Make working together a priority.

As soon as there is more than one carer in your young child's life, do what you can to facilitate working together as this is more effective.

❷ Do not change just for the sake of it.

Stick to your own ideas about your child's behaviour and the way it should be managed unless the others involved offer good reasons for change.

Listen and Learn

A key strategy for sharing ideas effectively with all your child's carers is to listen to their perspectives and then discuss a suitable way forward. While you may not always agree with them initially, there is no harm in listening to what they have to say – if they have a lot of childcare experience, you may find their advice and opinions reassuring and helpful. You might be persuaded or learn something new. In the end, however, you will decide how your child should be raised.

behave. This can be hard to achieve, but it is worth the effort.

Regular Reviews

Once you have reached agreement on childcare strategies, monitor the effectiveness of this approach. Set a time – say, four weeks later – when you will meet with the other people caring for your child to discuss how the arrangements are progressing. Regular monitoring and reviewing of the way all the adults in your child's life link with each other enables consistency to be achieved.

Minor difficulties are dealt with before they become major, so that your child experiences stability from all his carers.

Varied Activities

Remember that you don't all have to do everything with your child. For instance, not every carer has to take him to the park, play a board game with him, read him a story, put him to bed and so on. It often makes more sense for some child-related tasks to be allocated to one carer and not the others, depending on the amount of time they spend together. There will always be overlap between the roles of different carers, but allocating separate tasks to the individual adults who look after him could mean that your child receives a more stimulating daily programme of activities.

Making time to talk to your child's carers regularly will help you assess how things are going.

❸ Involve your child.

He will appreciate being told that you and his other carers have had a chat together. Reassure him that you all know what the others do with him during the day.

❹ Be willing to adapt.

You won't always be the one who has the best ideas about bringing up your child. Others will have learned from experience, and you may need to adapt.

❺ Resolve disagreements.

If there is a disagreement between you and another of your child's carers, sort it out as quickly as possible – your child dislikes any form of adult disagreement.

Be Flexible

There is no one 'right' way to bring up a child so that she is well-behaved. True, some parenting rules apply to all children: for instance, the rule that they should be loved and the rule that they should not live in fear of physical or emotional abuse. These are principles with which no sensible parent would disagree. Beyond these, most dimensions of parenting are open to debate.

Individual Differences

Take the simple issue of positive reinforcement. Your youngest child might respond best when promised an extra story at bedtime – this could be just the incentive she needs to motivate her to improve her behaviour. Yet when your oldest child was the same age, she might have been totally unmoved by the promise of an extra bedtime story – perhaps she only responded positively when the incentive involved having extra time to play with her friend. Children's interests and individual characteristics influence the way you relate to them. Different children within the same family often require subtly different parenting approaches.

Age Differences

Your child's emotional needs change with age. A simple cuddle and a few words of reassurance are often sufficient to restore the confidence of a toddler who has been rejected by her peers, while a more mature 5-year-old in the same situation probably requires specific advice about how to improve her social skills or resolve conflict with her friends. To be effective, your parenting techniques need to adapt as your child grows older.

Finding the right way to deal with emotional upset is one of the most important aspects of parenting.

5 Top Tips

❶ Evaluate your methods.
Consider the different strategies you use to manage your child's behaviour and regularly ask yourself whether or not these techniques are still effective.

❷ Look for progress.
If an approach you use for handling an aspect of your child's behaviour does not achieve success, then perhaps it is time to accept that this approach isn't right for her.

The kind of attention children need may differ markedly according to age, temperament and environment.

Dynamic Differences

Parents can even find that a strategy for managing their child's behaviour that worked last week has reduced impact or doesn't work this week. Interactions between parent and child are dynamic and fluid. For example, your infant cries during the night: the first time, you lift her up, cuddle her, give her a drink and then settle her back into her cot or bed. That's a perfectly reasonable, caring parental approach to a crying infant who has woken during the night as the result of a bad dream. Suppose she has another bad dream the next week and you run through the same comforting process. Again, that is perfectly reasonable.

But the situation changes subtly if your child wakes up during the night a third time, not because she has had a bad dream but because she has learned that waking up during the night results in a cuddle, a game and an extra drink – in other words, she now thinks night waking is good fun! To continue with your previous strategy is no longer appropriate, because it perpetuates the behaviour you want to prevent. Now, the more you play with her when she wakes, the more likely she is to wake the next night, too. You could now decide to be less responsive during future episodes of night waking, possibly by calming her but keeping her in her cot without any further stimulation.

Through this process, your parenting approaches and your child's behaviour have meshed, altered each other, and are different from the way they were before the very first episode of night waking. This is further evidence of the need for flexibility in parenting.

❸ Use your judgement.

Do not try out a particular approach just because your best friend assures you that it works with her child. Weigh up the suitability of this for your child.

❹ Accept flexibility.

If you have applied a strategy for managing her behaviour consistently for several weeks and there has been no change, try something else.

❺ Use your accumulated understanding.

When interacting with your child, use your existing knowledge of her likes and dislikes, strengths and weaknesses, to identify appropriate strategies.

Cause for Concern

Most parents worry about their child's behaviour sometimes and may be unsure whether it is normal or so extreme that it has become abnormal. It is important to know the difference, but reaching that understanding is not easy.

What is Normal?

First, you need to realize that a lot of normal child behaviour is challenging, and a lot of challenging behaviour is normal. Let's look more closely at what this actually means.

Tantrums

Toddler tantrums, for example, are often absolutely draining to manage. Coping with the rage of a furious 2-year-old leaves you exhausted, pessimistic, tense and worried, but toddler tantrums are normal – yes, they are challenging, annoying, fierce and upsetting, but normal all the same.

Tantrums are normal – they occur in the majority of children of this age. The fact that your toddler's rages push you to your limits and even beyond does not mean that they are abnormal behaviour. On the contrary, you would be hard-pushed to find a parent whose 2-year-old does not have such outbursts.

Knowing that your child's explosions are normal doesn't make them any easier to handle, yet that knowledge should provide you with reassurance that this sort of behaviour is almost completely universal and therefore not at all abnormal.

Tantrums can be daunting but the key to getting through this phase is to develop a strategy for managing them firmly and calmly.

5 Top Tips

❶ Stay calm.

A one-off episode of behaviour from your child does not mean that he is abnormal. Try to stay calm. Wait to see if it is repeated before worrying about abnormality.

❷ Aim for change.

Most child behaviour changes to some extent in response to parental efforts. It is only when the behaviour is completely resistant to any change that deeper concerns are justified.

Difficult Phases

In addition, children go through phases in their development when they are more challenging. For instance, a child may be socially confident for the first few years of his life and then suddenly become shy when he starts to attend nursery. You may have difficulties settling your 3-year-old there at first because he clings to you in tears, begging you not to leave him even though he played happily with others his own age until now. His shyness and reluctance to separate from you is due simply to the change in circumstances, and is a normal reaction. He will grow out of this shy phase within a few weeks as his confidence in the nursery grows.

Abnormal Behaviour

There are two main questions to ask in order to decide whether or not a child's behaviour is beyond the bounds of normality:

❶ **To what extent does the behaviour interfere with your child's everyday life and with the lives of others around him?** The greater the impact of his behaviour, the less likely it is to be normal. For example, many young children hit out in temper; this is a normal habit which should be discouraged from the beginning. However, if a child's hitting is so extreme that his parents receive constant complaints from nursery staff and other parents, and have to restrict his social life because he is so wild with his peers, then the impact of his behaviour on their lives suggests that his habit of hitting others is too extreme to be considered normal.

❷ **Is this behaviour typical for your child's age group?** For example, it is normal for a child aged 1 or 2 years to have a cuddly toy as a comforter, and he may take teddy to bed with him. He migh even take it on outings. It is unusual, however, for a 7-year-old to insist on taking a comforter to school and to cry hysterically if he is not allowed to. Behaviour that is not age-appropriate is less likely to be normal.

Keeping a diary may help you to identify if your child's behaviour is not normal. If you seek professional help these notes will be useful.

❸ **Build up your knowledge base.**
You are better able to make judgements about behaviour when you have a good understanding of normal child development.

❹ **Recognize individual differences.**
Even though your child behaves differently from others, that does not automatically mean he is not normal. Every child is an individual, and there are wide differences within the normal range of development.

❺ **Remember that time matters.**
Difficult behaviour that is normal typically changes over time (although you still have to deal with it). Behaviour is more likely to be abnormal if it persists unchanged for months, or becomes more extreme.

Keeping a Strong Bond

The psychological and emotional bond you began to form with your baby early in her life grows in strength with each passing day, week and month. Bonds typically take time to develop and this process continues throughout her childhood.

Now she is less reliant on you for feeding, changing and stimulation – because she is active, mobile and alert – you cannot settle back and take bonding for granted. You must work hard to keep strong bonds, well beyond the first years.

Without continued secure emotional connections, your child's behaviour could become difficult to manage. She may become hard to handle, attention-seeking, disruptive and argumentative. This behaviour does not automatically signify a weak bond between you, but it can indicate relationship difficulties.

What You Can Do

You can help to maintain the psychological links between you and your child by continuing to show her that she matters to you and you value her and everything she does.

- **Keep in touch with all that goes on in your child's life.** The chances are you still have a busy schedule even though she is now at nursery, pre-school or perhaps school, while she attends many other activities outside the family home such as dancing classes, swimming or drama and spends time with her friends at their houses, too. This means that you

It is just as important to tell her how much you love her and to listen to her as she grows older.

5 Top Tips

❶ **Talk to your child.**
In most instances, she thrives under the glow of your interest and attention – although be aware that there will be moments when she prefers to sit silently when at home.

❷ **Verbalize your emotions.**
Just because she is older does not mean that she dislikes your loving comments. Tell her how much she means to you, and how much you like her.

Share his experiences outside the home – let him show you his project or tell you about his football match.

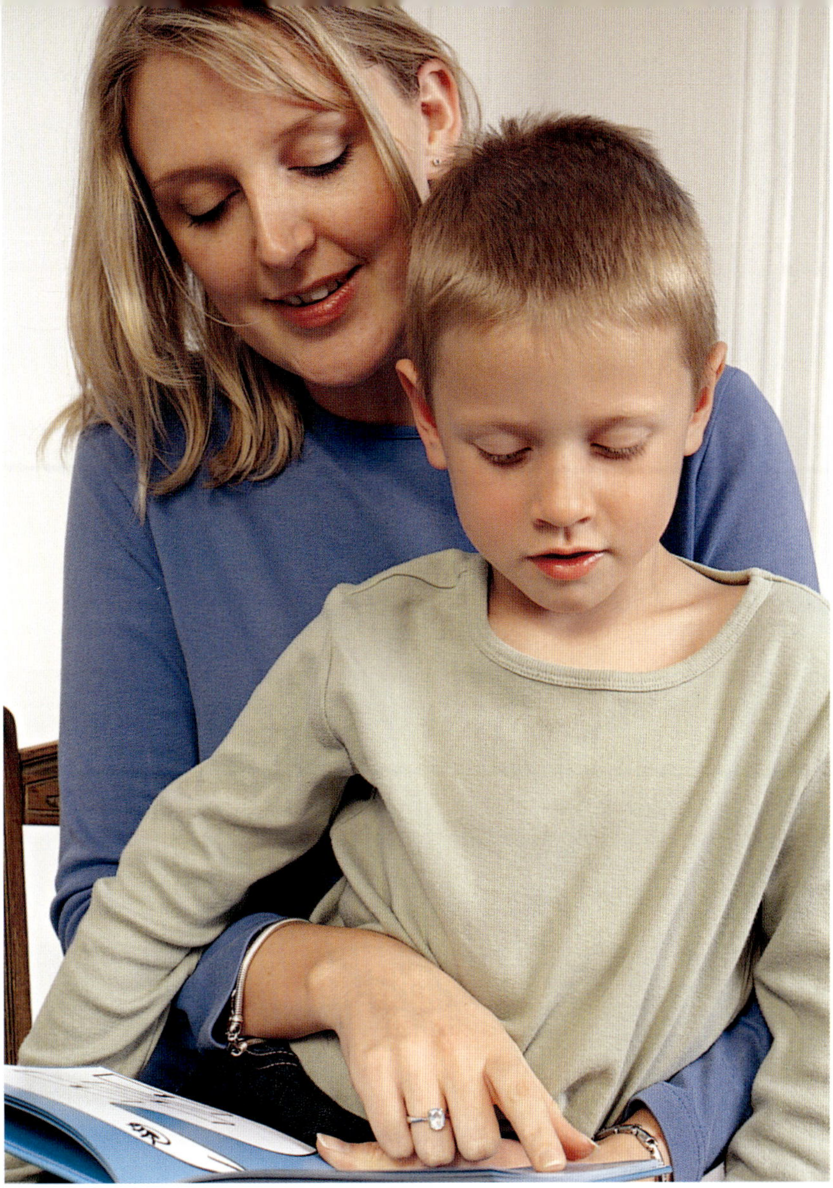

are not always in each other's company. That's fine – this change reflects progress in her development – as long as you show your genuine interest in her life. Ask her questions about activities, giving her advice, encouraging her progress, admiring her achievements and listening to her accounts.

- **Listen when she wants to express her feelings to you.** Make time to communicate with her so that she is able to talk to you freely about her emotions, ideas and hopes. Family life is rushed and you need to make an effort. Good communication between you cements your two-way relationship. Children can find it hard let go of babyhood and she may revert to babyish behaviour to get your attention.
- **Maintain closeness by comforting your child when she is upset.** She may give the impression that she is confident and independent, but she remains emotionally vulnerable throughout childhood. Your child needs you, no matter how self-sufficient she thinks she is. Be there for her if she is distressed. Loving concern and words of reassurance will help her get over this temporary setback. She will feel secure, knowing you are there for her and will come to you again in the future.
- **Share problem-solving challenges with your child.** By all means offer reassurance and comfort, but the bond between you grows stronger if you help her to solve her difficulties. For instance, if your child is distressed by a lack of friends, arrange an outing to which she can invite one or two other children. A simple, practical answer to a worry will boost her confidence in the parent-child bond.

❸ Respect your child.

The minor crises that she tackles each day are major as far as she is concerned. She feels better about her relationship with you when you respect her feelings.

❹ Give her lots of praise.

Do not hesitate to praise any progress that she makes. She values your approval, but equally try not to overdo it otherwise she may begin to doubt your sincerity.

❺ Enjoy joint activities.

No matter how busy you are, make a special effort to spend time every day in a shared activity with your child, perhaps playing or reading together.

rewards and controls

2 rewards and controls

- discipline styles
- not all negative
- responsibility for actions
- self-control
- persistent misbehaviour
- rewards and punishments
- star charts
- time out

Discipline Styles

By the time your child is born, you already have views about discipline. For instance, you might think that your crying baby should be left alone until he settles because that is the only way he will learn that there are rules. Alternatively, you may pick him up the moment he starts sobbing because you think there is plenty of time for him to learn about rules later on.

The way you think about discipline for your child is influenced by a number of factors, such as memories of your own upbringing, advice from other parents, friends and relatives, and observations of the ways in which other people manage their child's behaviour. Spend a moment or two of reflecting on these sources of influence. It is helpful for you to understand what the origins of your thoughts on discipline are.

Discipline Styles

Most styles of discipline fall into one of the following categories, although the chances are that your particular style is a mixture of at least two of these:

1. **Parent led.** With this style, the parents lay down the rules and there is no negotiation. Rules are fixed, immutable and must be followed at all times.
2. **Child led.** With this style, the child is allowed to determine the rules by himself. He sets the limits of his own behaviour, and learns through experience.
3. **Parent-child led.** With this style, rules are explained by the parents but can be negotiated to some extent by the child himself once he is a little older.

Easy to use furniture, like this low-level coat stand, will encourage your child to put his own things away.

5 Top Tips

1. **Keep rules simple.**
The more basic the rule, the better. First, your child understands it more easily. Second, there is less ambiguity – there is no room for him to interpret the rule in his own distinctive way.

2. **Check his understanding.**
One way to verify your child's understanding of a rule is to ask him to explain it to you. You can then tell by the quality of his response whether or not he really understands what the rule is about.

A little more flexibility is often required in disciplining older children but consistency and fairness are still vital.

Internalizing the Rules

Your underlying aim should be to encourage your child to develop self-discipline, to 'internalize' the rules. In other words, he should reach the point where he knows the rules himself and follows them without any instructions from you. Self-discipline can only occur when rules are fully explained to your child – without understanding why he should behave in a particular way, he may behave when he is under your supervision but will probably misbehave the moment you stop watching him. Give him lots of praise when you see that he behaved appropriately without you having to remind him.

Findings from psychological research indicate that typically discipline is most effective when it is parent-child led, because the child is encouraged to understand the purpose of behavioural rules from an early age and also has some degree of control over them. Choose the style that best suits you and your child.

Changes with Age

Bear in mind that your style of discipline will change as your child develops, for several reasons. First, you build up experience and learn which approach works best with him. Second, his understanding develops as he grows older – for instance, it makes sense to reason with your child about his behaviour when he is 8 years old, but the same approach is not so appropriate when he is 18 months old.

Most parents increase their flexibility with discipline as their child matures, because they have greater trust in his ability to interpret rules and to make good judgements by himself. There is no problem with this. However, no matter what age he is your child still needs you to take a consistent approach with discipline. He thrives best with stability, so any changes you make to the rules governing his behaviour should be small and gradual.

❸ Justify rules to yourself.

There should be a good reason for having a specific rule. If you cannot offer a acceptable justification for it, then perhaps it is time to consider changing it.

❹ Make rules explicit.

You know how your child should behave but he might not. Tell him your expectations at the outset: don't wait until he breaks a rule before explaining it to him.

❺ Be flexible.

There are very few rules about behaviour that cannot be adapted. There is no harm in bending the rules sometimes – for instance, varying bedtime when it is a special occasion. Explain why you are relaxing the rule on this occasion so that he does not expect it to be bent every time.

Not All Negative

Of course, a large part of discipline involves teaching your child rules, but the process need not be entirely negative. In fact, positive discipline is much more enjoyable for both you and your child. Here are some strategies for establishing a positive approach to discipline at home.

- **Highlight examples of good behaviour.** Instead of telling your child off when she behaves badly, give her lots of praise when she behaves well. Tell her, for example, that you were happy with the way she helped her friend with her homework. Your child thrives under your approval.
- **State rules positively.** The problem with a rule that starts 'Don't...' is that it only advises your child what not to do – it doesn't actually point out to her what she should do. Negative 'Don't...' rules also create a somewhat sour atmosphere, so try to have rules without the words 'not' or 'don't' in them.
- **Ask your child's opinion about the rules.** Involving her in understanding – even planning – rules makes her feel part of the process. From the age of 3 or 4 years onwards, you can start to have discussions with her about why rules matter and she can suggest some rules herself.
- **Find positives every day.** No matter how trying a day you have had, find something about her behaviour that you can praise. Sometimes you might have to dig deep to find an instance that merits your enthusiasm, but do it anyway! It's always good to end each day on a positive note.

Praising your child's achievements will increase her self-esteem.

5 Top Tips

❶ Keep punishments small and rewards big.

It is far better to be over-enthusiastic about rewards than about punishments, although children respond better to moderation than they do to extremes.

❷ Have an end-of-day summary.

Take a couple of minutes with your child at the end of each day to review her behaviour. Do this when you are both calm and less rushed.

Finding something to be positive about is a good way to end the day.

Smacking Doesn't Work

Part of positive discipline is a commitment that you won't smack your child. Physical violence (and that is what a smack is, no matter how 'innocently' you describe it) hurts your child, makes her afraid and reduces her security with you. Any adult can bully any child into obedience with the use of physical punishment, but that's tyranny, not discipline.

There are a number of other reasons why you shouldn't smack your child. To start with, it doesn't work. There is not a shred of research evidence to show that a child who is smacked behaves better than a child who is not smacked. On the contrary, research has shown that children who are smacked at the age of 4 are usually still smacked at the same rate when they are 7 years old. In other words, smacking does not have any positive long-term impact on your child's behaviour.

After the short-term release of frustration when you smack your child, you will soon feel thoroughly miserable and disappointed. No parents likes to see their child look at them with fear in her eyes. That's certainly not a positive basis for establishing discipline. Moreover, smacking sets your child a bad example, by suggesting that violence is acceptable.

Speaking Positively

The language you use with your child has an effect on her behaviour and on the way she responds to your discipline. Try to frame criticism positively. For instance, instead of saying 'You are a horrible child for hitting your sister like that', you could use positive criticism and say 'I am surprised you hit your sister like that because you are usually such a lovely, caring child.' By setting her misbehaviour in a broader context of general praise, she is more likely to listen to what you tell her and is less likely to adopt a defensive attitude.

❸ Do not feel guilty.

Every parent takes action with their child that they later regret – nobody is perfect! If you over-reacted, say sorry: it's important for your child to realize that everyone can make mistakes.

❹ End confrontations quickly.

Once an incident of misbehaviour is over, leave it alone. Resist any temptation to keep referring back to it later in the day. Try to have a positive, forward-looking approach.

❺ Tell others.

When you have had a good day with your child in terms of her behaviour, let her hear you speak to her grandmother (or other relative) on the phone so that you can praise her to the hilt.

Responsibility for Actions

One of the key aims of your discipline strategy should be to teach your child to take responsibility for her own actions. You are already familiar with the plea 'but I didn't mean to do that', as if the fact that she didn't deliberately cause chaos gets her off the hook. Even worse is her outright denial of her misbehaviour when the reality is that you caught her red-handed.

An 8-year-old is as likely to disclaim responsibility for her actions as a 2-year-old, unless she has been taught to think otherwise. For your child to understand and accept the concept of 'ownership' of her behaviour, she has to:

- Recognize that her behaviour has an impact on people around her, and that the way she behaves creates a reaction.
- Admit that her behaviour is within her control, that she can make choices about the way she behaves and following rules.
- Be prepared to recognize the consequences of her behaviour and to make amends.

Life is a lot easier for your child when she does not have ownership of her behaviour. There is no responsibility, no commitment and no need to think ahead. Hardly surprising, then, that she would prefer to leave ownership with you.

What You Can Do

The first step in teaching your child to take responsibility for her own behaviour is by drawing explicit links between one of her actions and the resulting reward or punishment. That's why your responses to her behaviour should be immediate.

Once you have issued a punishment (in this case the withdrawal of a video) you must remain firm.

5 Top Tips

❶ Encourage sensitivity.

Ask your child to think about the feelings of those people affected by her actions. Expect more than her usual 'I don't know' response to your questions.

❷ Always explain punishments and rewards.

Never give a reward or punishment without an accompanying explanation. You cannot be sure that your child sees the connection between her behaviour and your response.

A child who knowingly does something wrong must understand that she is responsible for her behaviour and its consequences.

Depending on your child's age, a lengthy time delay between her behaviour and the reward or punishment might mean that she fails to see the connection between the two, and will not develop a sense of responsibility for her actions. As a rough guide, the delay between her behaviour and your response should be no more than seconds when she is 2 years old, minutes when she is 4 years old and hours when she is 7 or 8 years old.

Always give an explanation for the reward or punishment you deliver to your child. She cannot start to take responsibility for her behaviour until she understands the reasoning underlying your reaction. Make no assumptions about this – spell it out clearly. For instance, say to her 'The reason I am not letting you watch your favourite video now is because you just lost your temper with your little brother.' This may seem obvious to you, but it might not be so clear to your child. The more you emphasize the links, the better.

Warning Your Child

Responsibility goes hand-in-hand with choice, so try to give your child some warning of the implications of her behaviour. Then she can make a choice (to some extent) as to whether or not she follows the rules you set out. For instance, say to her 'If you bump against the table once more, I'm going to send you out of the room.' Then, if she does bump into the table again, say to her 'I'm sending you out of the room because you bumped into the table, just as I said I would.' Giving this kind of warning forces your child to take responsibility for her behaviour.

❸ Match punishments to the misbehaviour.

Your child will never take responsibility if your reaction is too extreme. Instead, she will devote all her efforts to concealing the misbehaviour.

❹ Keep rules consistent.

Another benefit of having a consistent, structured approached to discipline is that your child learns to predict accurately your reaction to any of her inappropriate actions.

❺ Make amends.

If possible, find ways in which your child can make amends for her misbehaviour. For instance, she can make a verbal apology to a child whose toy she broke.

Self-Control

One of the major challenges facing your child is the task of gaining control over her feelings, thoughts and behaviour. From the age of 2 or 3 years onwards, people expect her to act less impulsively and to think about others. Without self-control, her relationships become strained and unpopularity sets in.

Bear in mind that in the long term she, not you, should be responsible for behaviour. This means that reprimanding her severely every time she misbehaves should not be your first reaction, because that involves you taking charge of her behaviour. She has to take charge herself, and develop a range of useful techniques that she (not you) can use to improve her self-control.

Dealing with Lapses

No matter how much you try to teach your child self-control, there will be moments when she forgets all you have taught her – she is only human, after all. Don't make too much out of these occasional lapses in self-control and do your best not to over-react. The chances are that she is just as disappointed as you are to find herself in hot water once again because of her misbehaviour. Deal with these episodes briefly and quickly as they arise, then make no further reference to them. As your child grows older, these temporary lapses in her self-control will become less frequent.

Small children are easily upset – you need to be understanding as well as helping them gain self-control.

5 Top Tips

❶ Be sympathetic.

A small incident can cause your child to lose self-control. A poor grade in a school test or distress at not getting invited to a friend's party can really unsettle her.

❷ Use delaying tactics.

You can help your child gain self-control by suggesting that she counts to ten before reacting. This delaying tactic gives her time to think before she acts.

Older children also need help to control their behaviour. Be aware of any underlying stress.

- **Teach awareness.** Make your child aware of other people's feelings. Remind her that her behaviour has an effect on others. She will be more motivated to gain control once she fully understands that lack of self-control has negative effects on the people she cares about.
- **Encourage reflection.** Help her to think before she acts. This is very difficult for an excited child to achieve – her natural tendency is to respond to her urges the moment they arise. Suggest to her that she waits for a second or two before reacting.
- **Monitor progress.** Watch to identify when she behaves maturely instead of giving in to her first impulses. For example, give her lots of praise when you see her successfully control her temper if teased by a sibling.

Respecting House Rules

It is perfectly reasonable for you to expect your child to respect your house rules (assuming that they are sensible, fair and reasonable). When your child does challenge a standard of behaviour at home, stick to your principles. Do not give in just for the sake of a quiet life. Although it might be easier for you to let her do what she wants – because that way she will calm down – in the long run this strategy will backfire on you.

Set out your house rules as clearly as you can, and show your displeasure when your child breaches them. Explain the reasons for each rule, setting out the negative effects when she breaks it. Point out to her that these rules also benefit her – for instance, the 'no hitting' rule means that she does not have to worry about slaps and kicks from her siblings. She becomes more respectful of your house rules when she realizes that they have advantages for her, too.

❸ Set a good example.
You cannot reasonably expect your growing child to control her behaviour when she watches you fly off the handle the moment things don't go your way.

❹ Signpost the positives.
Explain to your child the positive impact of her self-control. For example, remind her that her friends enjoy her company when she behaves predictably.

❺ Help her to find solutions.
When she misbehaves and then finds herself in trouble yet again, ask her to think of ways this situation could have been avoided. She may be able to identify her own solutions.

Persistent Misbehaviour

Repeated misbehaviour from your child can drive you to distraction – the constant touching of fragile objects by your 2-year-old, or the continued moans from your 7-year-old when you ask him to tidy up, can be a cause of frustration and annoyance.

The failure of your small-scale punishments tempts you to escalate their size, intensity and length. Whereas the first time you punished your child's misbehaviour with, say, denial of sweets that afternoon, by the tenth time he misbehaves you feel you would like to punish him by never letting him have any sweets ever again!

However, it is important for the punishment to fit the 'crime', not your anger. Just as adults are not hanged for parking offences (even

5 Top Tips

❶ **Have a prearranged list.**

To make life easier for yourself, compile a list of punishments for common acts of misbehaviour: for instance, hitting his young brother means going to bed ten minutes early that night.

❷ **Listen to explanations.**

Give your child a chance to speak to you. He may have a perfectly good explanation for his actions, even though you are unhappy with his behaviour.

though their poor parking may have had a severely disruptive effect on the traffic), neither should your child be dreadfully punished for a minor misdemeanour (even though his actions triggered your own temper). If there is a mismatch between your child's misbehaviour and the scale of your response, he will have difficulty making sense of your discipline system.

Intention not Outcome

You know that the intention underlying an action is more important than the outcome – for instance, it is less of a 'crime' when your child accidentally drops his entire bowl of milk and breakfast cereal on the floor than it is when he deliberately flicks a spoonful from his plate on to the floor. Human nature, however, means that you might impulsively punish your child for the outcome and not for the underlying intention. That's why it is good for you to think before you punish. Consider your child's motives and perception of his behaviour and take that into account before embarking on your response.

Children may encourage each other to misbehave, so ensure that your child's friends know your rules.

Squabbles are very frequent – getting one or both children to apologise can diffuse the situation.

Wherever possible, match misbehaviour and punishment thematically. For instance, if your child breaks his friend's toy in temper, he should replace it with one of his own; if he takes his sister's sweets without permission, he should make amends by giving her some of his sweets. Although not always possible to achieve, this thematic linkage is very effective.

Consistency

Of course, you have to be flexible when it comes to your child's behaviour. Much depends on the circumstances and context of each specific incident. In addition, you have to bend the rules occasionally, perhaps if his negative behaviour is in response to provocation by another child. In general, however, aim for consistency in your approach to punishment.

Parents often become disheartened when they punish their child for misbehaving and then he repeats the action a few minutes later. This leads to self-doubt and the belief that their system of discipline does not work – after all, they reason, their child wouldn't misbehave if they themselves were effective parents. As a result, they try something else the next day when their child continues to act inappropriately, and when that does not immediately have the desired effect, they try something else.

This shift from one strategy to another destroys any pattern of consistency, reducing the potential benefit of the techniques. Give your system of discipline, your use of rewards and punishments, time to work. In general, you should persist with a management technique for two or three weeks before giving up on it. Consistency is crucial for your child to achieve self-control, and he cannot reach that target when you change your approach from one day to the next.

❸ Vary the punishments.
Be ready to 'mix and match' from your prearranged list. A punishment that appears to have an effect on your growing child one day might not have the same effect a week later.

❹ Learn from other parents.
Each parent uses their own system of punishments. You can learn about other possibilities by talking to your friends about their approaches.

❶ Check out your child's understanding.
When the punishment episode is over, chat to your child to make sure he knows that this incident has finished. Restore a positive atmosphere.

strategy: Rewards and Punishment

Most parents are tempted at first to manage their child's behaviour more through punishments than rewards, because it's easier to react quickly to misbehaviour than to good behaviour. However, you should try to make the effort required to rely more on rewards.

Pros and Cons

There are several reasons why rewards are a more effective strategy for managing your child's behaviour. They are usually better because they:

- Focus on your child's appropriate behaviour.
- Are fun to give and to receive.
- Cement the relationship between you and your child.
- Boost your child's self-esteem.

In contrast, punishments:

- Focus on your child's inappropriate behaviour.
- Are unpleasant to give and receive.
- Weaken the relationship between you and your child.
- Reduce your child's self-esteem.

Tangible Rewards

You want your child to behave out of respect and consideration for other people – not simply to get a reward. If she behaves only to receive a promised reward, there is no reason for her to continue to behave once she has received it. That's why psychologists have found that behaviour-change programmes based solely on a tangible reward system rarely achieve any more than a temporary effect – the original misbehaviour returns soon after the rewards stop.

Instead, encourage your child to behave because of the pleasure she receives from showing thoughtfulness to her friends. She behaves more responsibly when she values herself, other people and her relationships with them. You can achieve this more effectively through discussion and explanation than through promises of, presents, money or treats.

The Concept of 'Extinction'

You may inadvertently reinforce your child's misbehaviour through your reaction to it. For instance, suppose that every time she touches an item in the supermarket during a shopping trip you stop, pick her up, reprimand her for several seconds, then insist on holding her hand so that she stays close to you.

What you may not realize is that your response could actually reinforce her misbehaviour because it means you are no longer ignoring her – she learns that touching objects in the shop grabs your attention. Ignoring her misbehaviour can make it 'extinct', because your lack of response makes her misbehaviour less attractive from her point of view. This tactic doesn't always work but is worth considering.

Time to Say 'No'

No matter how much you intend to avoid setting fixed rules and using punishments, and to encourage a positive approach to discipline, there are times when you have to lay down the law instantly. These moments are typically to do with safety, for example:

- Your 2-year-old is about to drink fluid from a bottle under the kitchen sink.
- Your 4-year-old is about to ride her three-wheeler into the main road.
- Your 6-year-old is about to punch her brother or sister.
- Your 8-year-old is about to experiment with pushing a small toy into an electric socket.

Rewards need to be used carefully – you want your child to learn good behaviour for its own sake.

Questions and Answers

Our 3-year-old won't eat vegetables. Is it good to promise her a reward for eating them?

No. The introduction of a reward can make the behaviour seem even more unattractive. She might think 'These vegetables must be ghastly or else mum wouldn't try so hard to persuade me to eat them.' A better approach is to purée a little of the vegetables, mix them into her main course and then – after she has cleared the plate – tell her how pleased you are that she has eaten the vegetables.

If a sharp smack stops my child's misbehaviour, what's wrong with that?

Physical punishment generates fear and self-loathing in your child, and it won't stop her from misbehaving when she is not under your immediate supervision. You will also find that persistent use of smacking makes her more aggressive. It encourages only blind obedience (through fear of pain), not a genuine understanding of your discipline system.

5 Practical Principles

1. **Time rewards carefully.**
   Never try to stop your child in the middle of an episode of misbehaviour by promising her a reward if she ceases to misbehave. She may expect a reward every time she misbehaves!

2. **Use rewards wisely.**
   Make sure there are times when you give your child a reward for her good behaviour even though she does not expect it.

3. **Keep rewards appropriate.**
   Try to avoid rewards that escalate too much in scale, or the rewards will become more important to her than the behaviour with which they are associated.

4. **Encourage reward-free behaviour.**
   Have times when you ask your child to do something for you without any promise of a reward.

5. **Reward effort.**
   Give your child a reward sometimes just because she tried hard to behave properly, whether or not she actually achieved her target.

strategy: Star Charts

A star chart is a simple technique that provides regular, visual incentives for good behaviour. Most star charts consists of a grid, with one column for each day of the week. Each day column is subdivided into three sections (morning, afternoon, evening) or into single hours (eight to nine, nine to ten, and so on).

How to Use a Star Chart

Each time your child behaves appropriately during a specific time period, you give her a little star to stick on that time slot in the grid. Her delight in achieving a star reinforces her good behaviour and encourages her to continue her good behaviour in order to get more stars on her chart. Star charts are useful from the ages of 2 or 3 years upwards.

Behaviour Contracts

For older children, perhaps aged 5 or 6 years upwards, a behaviour contract can be used. This is literally a written contract between you and your child that you both sign. The contract contains:

- The commitment your child gives: for example, to tidy her bedroom each night before going to sleep.
- The names of the people signing the agreement, typically you and your child, and their signatures.
- Any reward or incentive that your child obtains as a result of achieving the target set out in the contract.
- Any penalty or withdrawal of privileges your child receives if she does not manage to fulfil her part of the agreement.
- The way in which the contract will be monitored: for instance, you might decide to review your child's progress every day.
- The precise time and date that the contract starts and the precise time and date that the contract finishes (probably no more than one week at a time).

If you do use this type of written contract with your child, it is important that you both take it seriously. Give your child a copy (which she could display in her room) and keep a copy yourself. Chat to her each day about the behaviour spelled out in the agreement, giving positive encouragement whenever you can. At the end of the contract period, discuss with your child whether or not to start another one. You might both conclude that she can now control her behaviour without any further written support.

Questions and Answers

What is a behaviour diary?

Similar to a star chart, a behaviour diary is a basic way of recording your child's behaviour. At the end of each specified time period during the day, you write into the diary a description of your child's behaviour during that time. You then discuss this with her as soon afterwards as possible (so that she can remember what happened and why), whether the report is positive or negative. She keeps the diary to look at whenever she wants.

Surely star charts, contracts and behaviour diaries give you responsibility for your child's behaviour, not her?

That only happens if you do not use these strategies properly. In every instance, your child should be the one who has responsibility for reminding you to stick in a star or to complete the relevant part of the diary. Of course, you will do this if she forgets, but you should encourage her to remind you.

Star charts can give children a real sense of achievement if they are planned well and adhered to.

5 Practical Principles

❶ **Define 'good behaviour' very clearly.**
Your child needs to know exactly what you expect of her in order for her to achieve a star. Make it specific; 'sitting quietly without shouting' is better than 'behaving properly'.

❷ **Keep the chart visible.**
Make sure your child sees the chart throughout the day. Instead of keeping it in a drawer, you could stick it on a kitchen or bedroom wall.

❸ **Make a fuss.**
Since the whole point of the chart is to reinforce your child's good behaviour positively, create some pomp and ceremony each time she earns a star. This will add to the impact.

❹ **Use positive language.**
Don't use the phrase 'bad behaviour'. If she doesn't merit a star for a time period, say to her 'That's a pity, but I'm sure you'll get a star next time.'

❺ **Fill the chart regularly.**
Don't wait until the end of the day before allocating stars to the various time segments. Stick on the stars as soon as they have been earned.

strategy: Time Out

A popular strategy for responding to a child's negative behaviour is 'time out', in which your child is removed from the location of her misbehaviour and placed in a quiet area away from the scene of the conflict. It can be used for a whole range of misdemeanours, from mild through to more severe.

Time out helps children to calm down by removing them from the source of the conflict and taking the attention away from them.

Using Time Out

Time out is effective because it:

- **Reduces attention.** By taking your child away, she receives less attention for her misbehaviour. During time out, she only has an audience of one.
- **Removes the focus of the conflict.** Childhood arguments often centre around toys or siblings, and taking her to a different location places that source of conflict at a distance.
- **Provides a change of scene.** Behaviour is often context-bound and time out switches the physical context, which may change the behaviour (and in itself can have a calming effect).
- **Allows a breathing space.** The quiet atmosphere surrounding time out – even though it has arisen due to an increase in tension – is more likely to help your angry child settle down than leaving her at the point where the disagreement started.

For time out to be most effective it needs to be used appropriately, for example when your child persistently misbehaves or makes a frightful scene in front of other people. It can also be a good way of stopping your child fighting with a friend or sibling. Time out is not appropriate for situations which aren't your child's fault, such as toilet accidents or occasions when she is genuinely upset or frightened.

Age Suitability

Like all strategies to discourage disruptive behaviour, time out works best when your child is old enough to understand its purpose. Therefore, it is not recommended for a toddler under about 3 years old.

Questions and Answers

What should I do when my 5-year-old refuses to go to another room for time out?

At this age she is probably too big for you to carry her – and forceful physical pressure when she is in a temper is not advisable anyway, even if it is done with the best of intentions. Using a firm and stern tone, repeat your insistence that she walks with you to the designated area. If that fails, change the exact spot where she stands into the time-out area by removing the source of conflict: for instance, send the other children out of the room or take the toys elsewhere.

Is it acceptable to cuddle my 4-year-old during time out or should we sit silently together?

Of course you should give your child gentle, loving physical contact during time out if you find that helps her regain control. However, do not force this on her. Your child may respond better to a time out period when nothing is said or done to her. You will soon discover what suits your child best.

From then onwards, however, time out does make sense to your child. Explain to her that you are removing her because of her temper and in order to help her calm herself down. Emphasize that you want her to take control over her anger and you are doing this to help her achieve that target.

Once she is 5 or 6 years old, you may find that the threat alone of time out is enough to calm your raging child. Her increased self-awareness encourages her to heed your warnings, because she has learned from experience that you generally don't make empty threats.

5 Practical Principles

1. **Always stay with your child.**
   Never leave her alone during time out – if you do, you are giving her solitary confinement, not time out.

2. **Keep calm.**
   Losing your own temper will make matters worse. Be firm but calm, so that you provide a model of control she can copy.

3. **Pick a quiet area, free from distractions.**
   There is no point in removing her from, say, her bedroom into the living room where others are watching television.

4. **Set a time limit and stick to it.**
   Time out should last, at most, a few minutes. Whether she has calmed down or not at the end of the period, finish. Do not wait until she is completely calm or time out could last for an awfully long time.

5. **Repeat time out as often as necessary.**
   Be prepared to go through the same routine again and again until she becomes more responsive. For some children, the effect is cumulative rather than instant.

practical matters

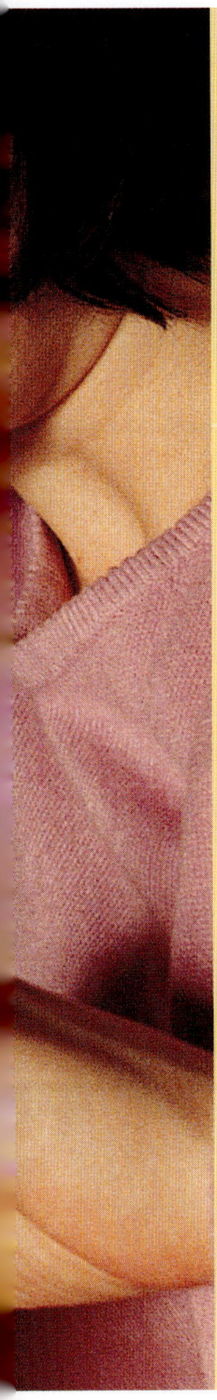

3 practical matters

Your 'Can-Do' Child

Every parent wants to raise a 'can-do' child – a child who stands head and shoulders above the rest because he approaches new challenges with great enthusiasm. It's not that he is foolhardy or reckless, just that he believes in his ability to do what is required.

The can-do child is also the one with a smile on his face who enjoys life to the full. He takes many of the normal, everyday hurdles that could create anxiety – such as meeting new friends, taking part in a new game in nursery, tidying his room, learning new topics in class – in his stride. Evidence from research suggests a child with a can-do attitude at the age of 5 years keeps this outlook into adulthood.

Key Strategies

It's great to watch your can-do child meet new hurdles and problems. He may start off with a frown, but within seconds he is working on a solution. Even if that particular approach flops, he simply tries again until he achieves his goal.

Here are some key strategies to help develop this type of upbeat attitude in your child:

- **Concentrate on his successes.** Draw your child's attention to his achievements. Of course, you should also acknowledge his failures, but don't dwell on them. It is far better to spend more time praising his successes.
- **Help him learn from his failures.** In many instances, your child fails at something the first

With encouragement and practical assistance you can help your child enjoy creative successes.

5 Top Tips

❶ **Support your child's efforts.** It's hard for him to keep going at an activity that is causing him to be frustrated. Be prepared to support him. Your words of encouragement could have considerable impact.

❷ **Subdivide challenges.** Success is easier to achieve when a problem is small. Teach your child to split any challenge into a series of smaller steps, each of which can be tackled individually.

Tell your child how proud you are when she learns a new skill, like riding without stabilisers.

time he tries it because of his approach. That's fine, as long as you help him learn from these occasions and direct him towards an alternative approach that leads to success.

- **Highlight his strengths.** The can-do child's enthusiasm for life and tackling new challenges rests on his conviction that he has the necessary skills to succeed. So highlight his strengths instead of dwelling on his weaknesses.

Be Realistic

Do not forget that no matter how strong your child's can-do outlook, there are limits to his possible achievements at each age. Part of your task is to encourage his determination but at the same time make sure he doesn't pitch his targets so high that he is bound to fail. There is no point, for instance, in giving your 2-year-old the challenge of tying his own shoe laces – he just doesn't have the manual skills and coordination required to complete the task.

When your child approaches a problem that is clearly beyond his capabilities, gently suggest that this would be difficult even for an older child. Then find him a hurdle that he could overcome. You will find that he is happy as long as he feels he has succeeded at something.

Can-Do 'Language'

The words you use to your child when he fails to meet an achievement target will influence his can-do attitude. Negative comments ('I'm disappointed in you') reinforce his sense of failure and are best avoided. Neutral comments ('We all have a bad day sometimes; believe me, you'll soon get over it') soften the blow by making an excuse for your child's lack of success, but this could make him feel worse. On the other hand, positive comments ('I know you are sad but I'm proud because you tried') acknowledge his failure but are helpful because they also offer encouragement and a way forward for the next time.

❸ Engineer successes.

It can be helpful to ensure your child achieves success occasionally, particularly if he has experienced a run of failures. Set him a task that is within his limits.

❹ Be a can-do parent.

Your child needs to see you make achievements, too. Explain to him how you cope with challenges by facing them head-on and searching for solutions each time.

❺ Give him ideas.

If possible, offer new solutions to your child when he thinks he is about to fail. One idea from you might trigger off a train of suggestions in his own mind.

Routines

As an adult, you may find that predictable routines bore you – perhaps you prefer variety. Your child likes variety, too, but she also benefits from having routines in her daily activities.

Consider these advantages of routine for your child:

- **Advance planning.** Your child is happy knowing that she goes to nursery every morning, or that when she comes home from school she has a snack while watching television. In this way, routine helps her to plan ahead. She can organize her activities around her routine so that she gets the best out of each day.
- **Consistency.** Your child thrives best in a consistent environment. Of course, she likes change and excitement, but a routine fulfils her deep-rooted psychological need for stability. Routine provides a secure foundation on which to build her daily activities.
- **Control.** If she has some choice in her routine – for example, she is allowed to choose when to play with toys or read a book – this predictable framework allows her to have some degree of control over her world. This is a terrific boost to her self-esteem.

Keeping to Routines

It's one thing to have routines, but it's quite another to encourage your excitable child to follow them! You can increase her commitment to routines by explaining their underlying purpose. For instance,

Help your child prepare for outings by letting her know in advance.

5 Top Tips

❶ Warn in advance.

If you know there is an impending change in your child's routine that morning or afternoon, tell her in plenty of time so that she is able to adjust her expectations.

❷ Introduce changes.

The longer a routine has been in place, the more difficult it is for your child to accept an alteration. That's why it can be helpful occasionally to introduce variations deliberately.

An older child can take some reponsibility for planning her day, by packing her bag for example.

it's better to tell her 'I want you to do your homework now as usual, because I think you will be too tired later on in the evening' than to say 'Do your homework now because I'm telling you to.' The more she understands why the routine exists, the more likely she is to follow it.

Unexpected Changes

Once your child is used to routines, she could become unsettled by any sudden and unexpected changes – for instance, due to the cancellation of a leisure class or the onset of bad weather. In these circumstances, calm her, acknowledge her disappointment and reassure her. Then between you, decide on an alternative activity to replace the cancellation and make sure she launches into that with full enthusiasm. Learning to cope with unexpected changes is part of the process of growing up. Your child will learn to handle these minor interruptions to her otherwise organized life as her confidence steadily builds through experience.

Encourage your child to anticipate the next stage in her routine. For instance, during the morning remind her what the routine holds for her in the afternoon. Talk about the next part of the routine positively.

'I Want a Change'

Do not dismiss her complaints out of hand. If she insists that she is bored with her regular routine, ask her to consider ways in which it could reasonably be changed. For instance, there is no law that says she must play with her friends at a certain time each day. Ask her to suggest alternative ways in which her day could be organized.

If you agree to changes in her routine as a result, do what you can to stick to them. Emphasize that you support her suggestions and that you expect her to adhere to them. She will be more satisfied with routines when she feels that she has played her part in forming them.

❸ Don't be a slave to routines.

If you reach a stage where both you and your child are fed up with same old routine each time, then it's time to think seriously about change.

❹ Discuss routines.

At the end of the day, chat to your child about her activities. Listen to her comments and make positive remarks about the next time she will repeat those activities.

❺ Use routines to your advantage.

For example, if you know that your toddler has a long nap every afternoon at a specific hour, use that time to do something that suits you.

Making Decisions

You spend your life protecting your child, and making decisions that ensure her best interests. Yet you can't make all her decisions for her forever – it is better to encourage your child to become involved in simple decisions from an early age, as this prepares her for making more complicated ones later on. Even a toddler can choose between two different toys or two sweets.

Build Up Slowly

Start off small. Build up your child's confidence and decision-making skills slowly by allowing her to make minor choices in her life. For instance, let her choose between two breakfast cereals or choose which jumper to wear. These are relatively unimportant judgements but they give your growing child early experience of making decisions, so that the process is easier the next time around. When she is trying to make decisions:

- Suggest that your child weighs up the pros and cons of each possibility very carefully.
- Discuss with her why she is more interested in this one than that one. Do this in a friendly, open way, otherwise your child will assume you are critical of her decisions.
- Let her explain the rationale behind her selection, even though you might not agree with the final choice she made.

Weighing up the facts like this – even when the decision appears to be minor – helps your child to reach an informed choice, one that is based on her full awareness of the different alternatives that are available to her.

Children love being allowed to make simple decisions like choosing which piece of fruit to eat.

5 Top Tips

❶ Teach her to plan.

Every decision has a consequence for the decision maker. Discuss the potential outcomes of her choices – for instance, that buying a particular item could mean there is no money left for other things.

❷ Offer advice.

The decision may be hers but there is no harm in offering her your advice. As long as you frame your suggestion gently, she will listen and yet still make her own decision.

Letting your child make her own decisions boosts her confidence and tells her that her opinions matter.

Your reassurance on this point will increase your child's willingness to make up her mind about something and to do so with confidence. The more she makes these minor decisions, the more she will realize that nothing dreadful is going to happen as a result of her choice, and the more confident she will be about making decisions in future.

Boosting Confidence

Explain that making decisions is good fun and that she should not be afraid to make up her mind. This will boost her self-confidence, as she may worry that she will make the wrong choice and the other option would have been better.

Point out to your child that all the decisions she makes at this age – the television programme she would like to watch at home after school, the story she would like you to read to her at bedtime, the game she would like to play with her friend at lunchtime – are minor and are not likely to have serious consequences. So, she need not be afraid of making the 'wrong' choice because she can make a totally different selection the next time.

Approving Choices

When you let your child make a choice, you have to acknowledge the possibility that she might make an independent decision that is different from the choice you would really like her to make. This can be harder to accept than you might think. However, do your best to hide your disapproval in these circumstances. If you tell your child that she has a free choice, stick to your word. The only way she can learn how to make sensible choices in her life is by having opportunities to make up her own mind. Only tell her she has a choice when you are genuinely prepared to support whatever decision she makes.

❸ Don't say 'I told you so.'

Without doubt, there will be moments when she makes a decision that she later regrets. Reiterating your previous warnings does not make her feel any better about making a bad choice.

❹ Affirm her choice.

Once your child makes her minor decision, tell her that you are sure she made the right choice. She wants to hear your approval – so give it, despite any misgivings you may have.

❺ Encourage reflection.

Once a few days have elapsed since she made her decision, talk to her about its impact. Ask her to consider what the effect would have been of choosing the alternative.

Bedtime

Your child needs sleep every single day. If she doesn't get sufficient sleep and rest at night she will be irritable, uncooperative and moody. Sleep is essential for her satisfactory development, both physically and mentally. However, the fact that she needs sleep does not mean that she welcomes bedtime with open arms! In fact, you will probably discover that it is not until the school years that she views sleep positively.

Establishing a Routine

An important step in preparing your child for a good night's sleep is to develop a bedtime routine. The act of moving from a state of activity to a state of sleep involves a major shift in mood and behaviour. You cannot reasonably expect your dynamic child to switch her moods on and off like clockwork, to go from consciousness to sleep in an instant. Make sure the bedtime routine is enjoyable, so that it does not become a battleground.

Build up a series of steps that help to bridge the transition to bedtime and keep these in sequence. For instance, the steps might be to:

1. Tidy her toys away.
2. Have a bath.
3. Brush her teeth.
4. Put on her pyjamas.
5. Lie in bed while you read her a story.
6. Turn off the light.

The benefit of a bedtime routine is that it allows your child to calm down gradually, while preparing her physically for sleep at the same time. Her body gradually adapts to this routine so that the first step of it triggers off the first stage of relaxation. You may find that she

Sharing a story is a calm and relaxing way to end the day and wind down to bedtime.

5 Reasons why she won't go to bed

1 Staying awake is more fun.
The active mind of a young child would rather have stimulation than passivity. Small wonder, then, that your child asks to play for a few minutes longer when you suggest it is time for bed.

2 Life goes on when she is asleep.
Your child might resist bedtime and sleep because she is convinced that everyone else in the family has a good time without her. She wants to stay awake so that she doesn't miss out on any of the action.

starts yawning as she gets ready for a bath, even though bedtime is still many minutes away – her body has started to slow down automatically.

As you prepare your child for bed, aim for a steady reduction in stimulation. Remove potential distractions, such as toys lying on the floor – these could easily attract her attention. Turn down the volume on the television and radio. Have a calm manner as you interact with her, and talk in a quiet voice. These simple measures help the relaxation process unfold, so that sleep comes more quickly.

Your Child's Bedroom

The bedroom itself plays a huge part in determining her night-time behaviour. She will settle more easily into a sleep pattern when the bed is comfortable and inviting. Let her have a number of soft toys on her pillow so that she can cuddle them whenever she wants. If possible, involve your child in decisions about the wallpaper, the lighting and the choice of curtains.

Try to imagine what the bedroom feels like from your child's point view. Think about the ambient temperature, the distance from the bathroom, any background noises that are audible and even the comfort of the bed itself. If it doesn't seem friendly to you, then it definitely won't seem friendly to her. Unless she perceives the bedroom to be attractive and welcoming, she won't want to sleep there, night after night. Do what you can to make her bedroom desirable – that way, she will look forward to sleeping there.

Involving your child in choosing her own duvet cover or curtains will help her feel the bedroom is her own space.

❸ She doesn't understand the significance of sleep.

The link between her irritability and her tiredness may not be obvious to your child. That's why you need to point out the connection so that she understands why sleep matters.

❹ Her bedroom is unattractive.

She sleeps best in comfortable surroundings. If the room is too cold, too dark or the decoration is too dull, your child won't anticipate bedtime with any enthusiasm. Her bedroom should be attractive.

❺ Her mind is still racing.

She may still be thinking about the events of the day, and these images are so vivid and exciting that they keep her awake.

strategy: From Cot to Bed

At some stage – typically around the age of 2 years – you will need to consider moving your child from his cot to a 'big' bed. There is no 'right' time for this as much depends on your own attitude and on your child's level of maturity. However, most children have moved out of their cot and into a bed by the time they reach their third birthday.

With a bit of planning and the right approach, moving from a cot to a bed should be an exciting part of growing up for your child.

From your child's point of view, this is a huge step. He has been used to the safety and security of the cot since birth, and he loves it – the cot sides keep him safe, and the blankets and pillows are cuddly, warm and totally familiar. Compared to this security, a large bed with no sides, strange covers and lots of room can be quite intimidating for your growing child. That's why he may be apprehensive rather than excited about the proposed move.

When He Doesn't Settle

Be patient with your child – he needs time to settle in his new bed. Don't be surprised when he gets out of bed a couple of minutes after you tuck him in! He just finds it all a bit strange. Simply take him back to bed, sit with him once he is under the covers and perhaps read him a story.

You may have to take your child back to bed several times during the first few nights, but your efforts will soon pay off. Maintain a positive attitude: give him lots of praise for sleeping in his new bed like a 'big boy', and be sure to let him hear you announce this achievement to your friends and relatives.

Fear of the Dark

Most children are afraid of the dark sometimes. As well as calming him and explaining that he has nothing to fear, consider using the following strategy:

1. **Introduce a night light.** A small night light can help your anxious toddler overcome this temporary upset. There is no harm in using this device as a short-term arrangement until his confidence in the dark improves.
2. **Slowly reduce the night light.** As he feels more secure in the dark, slowly reduce the time for which the night light is switched on, until he no longer wants it on at all at bedtime. He gradually gets used to the dark.
3. **Take the night light away.** When he has slept through the night once or twice, quietly remove the night light altogether. In its place, leave a small light on in the hallway outside his room.

Questions and Answers

Our 3-year-old is in his own bed, but he still wants to have the cot blanket from his old bed. Should we allow this?

Yes, you should. There is no reason why not – in fact, this could be very positive. Using his cot blanket can help bridge the transition phase from cot to bed. The blanket is familiar and reassuring to your child. Its very presence calms him down when he's in his new bed and helps him to fall asleep.

When should we take the old cot away? We still have it in his bedroom because he likes it there alongside his bed.

Tell your child that the cot will be taken away two days from now because there is no longer enough room in his bedroom. He could help to dismantle it, or he may prefer it to be removed in his absence. Within a couple of days, he won't even remember the cot was ever there. He will also be pleased at having more floor space for playing with his toys.

5 Practical Principles

1. **Discuss the move with your child in advance.**
Explain the process to him ahead of the move, so that he has time to adjust to the idea of change.

2. **Play the 'big boy' card.**
Point out that 'big boys' sleep in a big bed – this acts as an incentive. He wants to be like an older child.

3. **Let him choose.**
If possible, involve your child in decisions about the bed, the covers, the pillow and so on. This harnesses his enthusiasm from the start.

4. **Position the bed in advance.**
Leave the bed in his room for a few days before he actually sleeps in it. This helps to build his confidence.

5. **Build up slowly.**
Start off with his day naps at first, then, once he is used to this, let him sleep in the bed at night.

strategy: Back to Bed

Surveys confirm that night waking – when a child wakes during the night at least two or three times every week – is one of the most common problems parents experience during the early years.

It is not difficult to understand why sleeping difficulties are so disruptive. First, a child who doesn't sleep well can be awkward to live with because of her irritability. Second, the cries of your sleepless child in the middle of the night wake you up – and perhaps your other children, too. Third, the negative effect of inadequate sleep is cumulative, making the problem worse with each additional day that passes.

Reducing Night Waking

Here are some strategies to settle your child when she wakes regularly:

- **Check that she isn't ill.** A child who is incubating an illness can have trouble getting to sleep several days before the first signs of the illness emerge.
- **Make her comfortable**. She needs to feel comfortable in her bedroom surroundings before she can fall asleep again.
- **Keep her in bed.** Although your child wakes, discourage her from actually getting out of bed.
- **Soothe her.** Comfort your child if she is distressed. Stroke her cheek and reassure her.
- **Do not play with her when she wakes at night.** Doing that will only make night waking more desirable from her point of view.
- **Stay with her until she falls asleep.** If necessary, remain with your child until she falls asleep. Leave the bedroom when she has dozed off again. The next night, leave a little earlier.

Children who wake regularly need to be settled back to bed with calm reassurance but without stimulation.

- **Repeat the process.** Go through all these steps for as many nights as you need, until the pattern of night waking is over – typically no more than six to eight weeks.

Nightmares

Most children have occasional nightmares, which distress them at the time – although don't be surprised to find that they remember nothing about the whole episode the following morning. Even very vivid nightmares – in which your child sits up in bed, cries loudly or actually shouts out – are typically forgotten by the time dawn breaks. Although these bad dream experiences are most upsetting for you to watch, they appear to be part of normal psychological development during childhood.

If your child has bad dreams that occur perhaps two or three times a week, look for possible causes. Sometimes these are triggered by eating a specific type of food (often cheese) just before bedtime, or by a child watching an unsuitable television programme or video in the evening. Nightmares can also be caused by anxiety – that's why you should check out what is happening in her life, perhaps at nursery, at school or with her friends. Once the trigger worry is removed, her dreams will become more pleasant.

Questions and Answers

Now that our 3-year-old is in her own bed, she gets up much earlier in the morning and wakes us all up. What should we do?

Encourage your child to stay in her own bed when she wakes in the morning. Keep a pile of toys and books by her bedside so that she can just reach out for them, without actually leaving the bedroom. This reduces her need to walk about the house in order to find something to keep her occupied.

Why does my child sleepwalk? She is 8 and she has done this every few months since she was 3 years old.

Psychologists and doctors cannot say why one child sleepwalks and another does not. No consistent personality patterns have emerged and a satisfactory explanation of this psychological phenomenon remains elusive. However, scientists have discovered that sleepwalking tends to run in families, which suggests that there may be a genetic component to the habit.

5 Practical Principles

1. **Stay calm.**
   To make sure your child does not stumble into anything and hurt herself when she sleepwalks, you need to stay calm and in control.

2. **Remove hazards.**
   You can keep your sleepwalker safe by moving floor furniture such as footstools and low tables out of the way every night.

3. **Make your house secure.**
   Close all internal doors and windows and lock the outside door at night. Maybe she could sleep on the ground floor.

4. **Steer your child back to bed.**
   Although she will probably return there herself, gently steer her to her bed, perhaps by softly turning her shoulders in the right direction.

5. **Never wake her.**
   Resist any urge to give her even a gentle shake during a sleepwalking episode – she is fast asleep.

Healthy Diet

Healthy eating habits start young. The moment you start weaning your baby on to solids foods, you need to think about ensuring she has a healthy diet. Your local health centre or family doctor will provide you with advice on the range of foods your child should eat at each age, in order to ensure satisfactory physical development. Try to keep these types of foods in mind when preparing her meals.

Obesity

Defined as the excess storage of fat, obesity is usually described as occurring when a child's weight is more than 20 per cent over the standard weight for her height. There is a link between obesity in childhood and adulthood – surveys indicate that 20 per cent of fat, overweight children become fat adults – and obesity in adulthood is associated with a whole range of health problems such as high blood pressure, diabetes, and heart and breathing problems.

In addition, fat children are often bullied by their peers, and this can lead to social rejection. Given the combination of physical and psychological problems connected with being overweight, it makes sense to avoid childhood obesity if at all possible.

There are two main causes of childhood obesity:

❶ **Possible inherited factors.** Studies have shown that when an adopted child is raised by obese parents, she is less likely to be obese than the natural children of these parents. In addition, if one identical twin is fat, the other tends to be of a similar weight although there is

Make fruit and vegetables a regular part of your child's daily diet.

5 Barriers to healthy eating

❶ **Repetition.**
Your child only wants to eat the foods she likes best. Give her a range of healthy foods alongside her favourites, not instead of them, so that she has the best of both worlds.

❷ **Convenience.**
She likes to eat finger foods that are easy to lift by hand. There is no reason why healthy foods cannot be convenient – sliced vegetables and fruit kept fresh in the fridge make a great snack.

Present healthy food so that it will appeal to your child, in a smart lunch box for example.

greater variation in weight in non-identical twins.

❷ **Not eating a healthy diet.** Over-consumption of foods with a high fat or sugar content (such as fried foods, junk food, sweets and biscuits), coupled with under-consumption of healthy foods (such as fruit, vegetables and fish), creates an environment in which obesity thrives. The current trend towards lack of regular exercise in childhood does not help.

There is no harm in weighing your child regularly in order to monitor her weight gain.

Additive Effects

Most modern packaged foods contain additives of one sort or another – these are natural or synthetic substances added to food either to preserve it for longer, to give it a stronger flavour or just to make it appear more attractive. Look at the contents labels on packaged foods: additives are those ingredients described variously as preservatives, stabilizers, flavourings, colourings and antioxidants.

The most common additives are identified by an 'E number': for example, tartrazine is E102 and sulphur dioxide is E220. It is rather frightening to think of all those chemicals as part of your child's diet, even if they are found in very small quantities.

There is evidence that additives can be linked to behaviour difficulties in childhood, particularly hyperactivity. Many parents and health professionals have found that when an overactive, impulsive child is placed on an additive-free diet, her difficult behaviour diminishes greatly. While this does not occur in every instance, there is too much evidence to ignore the suggested connection with additives.

That's why it is best to be fully aware of all the foods your child eats. Read contents labels very closely and try to avoid those with a long list of additives and E numbers. If you make the meal yourself instead of using processed foods, you will know exactly what has gone into it.

❸ **Hand control.**

Your child has genuine difficulty coordinating a knife and fork, so may prefer to snack on less healthy foods. Help her by letting her use one piece of cutlery at a time, then gradually encourage her to add a second one.

❹ **Independence.**

Once outside the family home, your child spends her money on sweets. Explain to her the damage that too many sweets can do and limit the amount of money you give her for treats and suggest she spends it on other foods such as cereal bars (but check the sugar content of these first).

❺ **Peer pressure.**

It might not be 'cool' for her friends to see her eating healthy foods, so try to make healthy foods more attractive. For instance, use them as sandwich fillings, put them in smart containers or wrap them in neat packages.

strategy: Avoiding Food Conflicts

Most children go through a 'fussy eating' phase in which they start to make stubborn choices about their food. Your child might demand the same meal night after night or she may eat much less than you expect. Food conflicts can be difficult to deal with, but it is important to prevent them becoming a confrontation.

Food cut into manageable pieces will seem more palatable to small children than whole items.

Bear in mind that you cannot force your child to eat what is placed in front of her. No matter how much pressure you put on her, she has to choose to eat. In fact, the more stressed she becomes, the less likely she is to eat, so challenging her about it will probably make the situation worse. Instead, a calm, planned approach is required. By all means try to persuade her, but the best solution to the problem might be to let her eat at her own pace.

Questions to Ask Yourself

❶ **Am I worried about my child's weight gain?** The most common concern about fussy eating habits is that the child won't thrive properly. So, have her weight checked by your family doctor – the chances are that her growth is fine.

❷ **Am I worried that my meals are wasted?** It's frustrating to spend a long time cooking, only to watch your child push the food around her plate. So, put less time and effort into food preparation, (but don't sacrifice quality) as this will reduce your irritation with her fussy eating.

❸ **Am I worried that there is a psychological problem?** Most fussy eaters grow out of this habit spontaneously. So, don't over-react, as this could actually increase the behaviour's attention-grabbing value for your child.

Questions and Answers

My child gets us so worked up about food that mealtimes usually end in tears. What can we do?

You need to force yourself to take a more relaxed approach to mealtimes. Since tension is highly infectious, you will make your child anxious before she sees the food. Try to hide your tension or the situation will not change. Chat calmly to your child while she eats, and set a good example yourself by eating whatever is on your plate.

Our child insists she will only eat snacks, and not proper plates of food. How can we overcome this?

Be creative. Identify the foods you want her to eat and then present them to her in snack format. For instance, if she barely touches a whole pizza that is put on a plate in front of her, simply cut it up into small pieces and serve these on a small side plate. Varying the presentation in this way makes the same food seem quite different, changing it from a formal meal into an informal snack.

Make Food Attractive

Look at the meal from your child's point of view. It has to be appealing or she won't have any desire to eat it. Here are some of food features that frequently depress a child's appetite:

- **Texture.** Food that is dry or greasy can stick to her upper palate, and may make her feel sick and possibly vomit.
- **Amount.** Don't pile her food high. Serve small portions on a large plate.
- **Heat.** Unlike adults, children generally prefer their food warm, not steaming hot.
- **Taste.** Your child is unlikely to enjoy spicy foods. She prefers bland tastes.

Practical Principles

❶ **Give your child some choice.**
She will be more interested in eating what is in front of her when she has selected it herself. If you can, let her pick from a very limited range of meal options – this boosts her mealtime motivation.

❷ **Involve her in preparing the meal.**
Much will depend on her age and stage of maturity: a 2-year-old can bring you potatoes from the larder, an 6-year-old can stir mixtures. Find some way to connect your child with the food preparation. The more she invests emotionally and physically in the meal, the more likely she is to eat it.

❸ **Offer small portions.**
Your child may be put off by a portion that seems very large, so offer a small portion at first and if she clears the plate she can have a second helping.

❹ **Introduce new tastes slowly and subtly.**
Start by mixing a small amount of the new food with something else, such as potatoes. Gradually increase the amount you disguise in this way. When your child eats this amount without comment, show her the new food and put a very small amount alongside her favourite food. Explain that she will find the taste familiar. Encourage her to try it and give her lots of praise when she puts some of it in her mouth.

❺ **Provide subtle positive reinforcement.**
Do not talk directly about how much she ate. Instead, at the end of the meal tell your child how much you enjoyed having a relaxed time with her.

strategy: Improving Table Manners

Nobody likes sitting at a table with a child who has disgusting eating habits! The sight of half-chewed food turning inside a gaping mouth puts most adults (and children) off their food, so start teaching your child table manners from an early age and explain the purpose of them. It's better to give him praise for good eating habits than to reprimand him for poor manners.

Here are some basic table manners that your child can learn during the early years:

- **Proper use of cutlery.** Encourage your child to hold his knife, fork and spoon suitably in each hand when eating a meal at a table.
- **Appropriate hand use.** Once he can use cutlery, discourage him from picking up food by hand during a meal, except bread and fruit.
- **Mouth position.** Strongly suggest that your child closes his mouth when chewing food – he may inadvertently let his jaw hang open while munching.

Mealtime Practice

Your child also learns good table manners through experience of family meals. Your family might have such a hectic schedule during the week that organizing a meal for everyone at the same time is an impossible

Family meals teach children that eating can be a social occasion and encourage good table manners.

task. Do your best, however, as this might be the only time that you and your family sit together during the entire week.

A family meal also provides a good opportunity for your child to practise his table manners and to learn new ones by imitating the behaviour of older siblings and adults. Other table habits, such as taking turns to speak in conversation, passing items to each other and listening while others talk also develop from the experience of family meals. Even if you are pressed for time because of the varying timetables of everyone at home, try to have a family meal for everyone at least once each week.

Questions and Answers

My child is 8 years old and he still struggles with full-sized cutlery. What should I do?

Let him continue to use child-sized cutlery until his hand control develops more fully. There is no point in simply insisting that he uses full-sized cutlery just because other children his age can manage these items in their hands. You will find that his hand control steadily improves with practice and maturity. You can reintroduce full-sized cutlery later.

Whenever I eat out with my child, he misbehaves through excitement and then we all end up in a bad mood. How can I change this?

First, do your best to calm him as you approach the restaurant; second, choose a restaurant that is full of children so that his excitement will go unnoticed. Your child's ability to control his behaviour will increase through experience, so the more you eat out together as a family the more he'll be able to cope with it calmly.

5 Practical Principles

Bad table manners can be particularly unwelcome if you and your family are eating out. Consider the following when you are planning to go to a restaurant.

1. **Pick a child-centred restaurant.**
   There is no point in taking your child to an expensive restaurant designed for adults on a large budget. Not only will he feel out of place in the over-formal surroundings, but he will not be made particularly welcome. In addition, the food will be too rich for him.

2. **Have realistic expectations.**
   You child is excited about the experience of eating out, and this means his appetite may decrease and his food selection may be inappropriate. Try to guide him in his choices, but don't be annoyed if he leaves the meal almost untouched on his plate.

3. **Prepare him for the restaurant food.**
   He likes your food because that is what he is used to eating every day; in addition, children are not very good at adapting to new eating experiences. Explain to your child that the restaurant food tastes different to the food at home.

4. **Emphasize the importance of table manners.**
   When you remind your child that there are others in the restaurant, he will begin to understand the social significance of table manners. Encourage him to watch the way the other customers eat. This reinforces his good table manners.

5. **Choose child-sized portions.**
   There is no point paying for huge portions when your child only has a small appetite. Contact the restaurant to check whether or not it serves child-sized meals or perhaps half-portions at reduced prices. It is wise to do this homework before you go to the restaurant.

Potty Training

Most parents begin potty training with their child at around 21 months, because by then the majority of children have sufficient neurological and muscle control to be successful. However, some children are not ready to come out of nappies until after their third birthday.

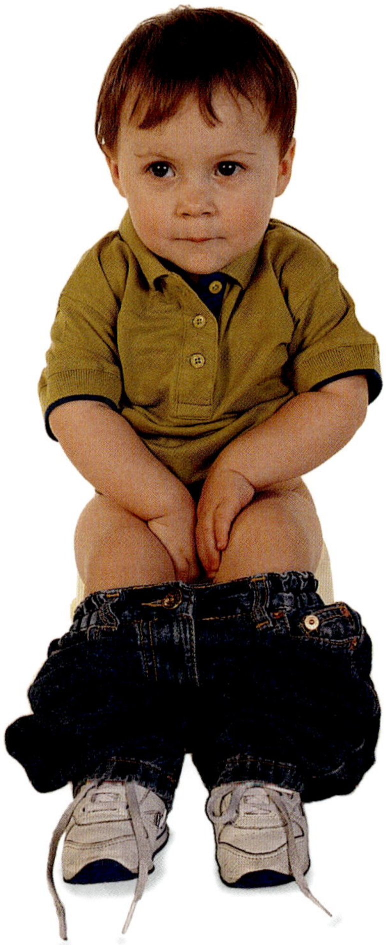

There are huge disadvantages associated with starting potty training too soon:

- You will be disappointed with your child's performance, and this negative attitude will show in the way you behave towards her. Your doubt about her abilities dents her self-confidence.
- You will create unnecessary frustration for both you and your child if you force her to reach standards that are much too high for her stage of development.
- You run the risk of putting her off potty training altogether, so that when she is actually ready her enthusiasm has already evaporated. Bear in mind, too, that children who start toilet training later tend to succeed more quickly anyway.

Facts About Toilet Training

- Almost 90 per cent of children gain reliable control over their bowel and bladder during the day by the time they reach the age of 3 years.
- A child will gain bowel and bladder control during the day first. Night-time control is usually established later.

Potty training is a big step forward for your child and he needs lots of patience and support.

5 Reasons for potty training battles

❶ Potty training starts too soon.
The child is simply not ready for this challenge and is being asked to achieve a skill that is physically beyond her. Wait until you think she is ready before beginning the training process.

❷ Parents expect too much, too quickly.
If expectations are unrealistically high that the child will gain full bladder and bowel control quickly, she will feel a failure. Allow her to move through training at her own speed.

- Occasional toilet 'accidents' are normal in a child who is reliably dry during the day. Ill-health, anxiety or poor timing will reduce her normal bladder control.
- Some parents claim that their child is potty trained at the age of 6 months. However, she only uses the potty automatically because she can't stand up and walk away from it.

Signs of Readiness

This is why you should wait until your child is ready – there are no advantages to early potty training, either emotional or psychological. Readiness varies from child to child, however. Here are some signs to indicate that yours may be ready for potty training:

- Her nappy is dry when you take it off, even though she has been wearing it for a few hours or more. This suggests she has some control over her bladder.
- She complains to you that her nappy is wet. This confirms that she can tell the difference between 'wet' and 'dry' – and she prefers to be dry!
- She asks not to wear a nappy. This suggests she has the underlying motivation to start potty training enthusiastically.
- When she wakes up from a brief daytime nap, you discover that her nappy is completely dry.

If your child seems anxious or upset, give her plenty of reassurance and praise every success.

Your Child's Perspective

In some instances, a child becomes upset by potty training because from her point of view:

- Her nappy is warm and comforting. She feels vulnerable and exposed without the thick, all-encompassing padding of the nappy.
- The sight of her body's waste material frightens or even disgusts her. She may be shocked to see that this material streams from her body.
- Wearing a nappy is easy. Emptying her bowels and bladder whenever she wants requires no effort whatsoever, unlike potty training which is more demanding.

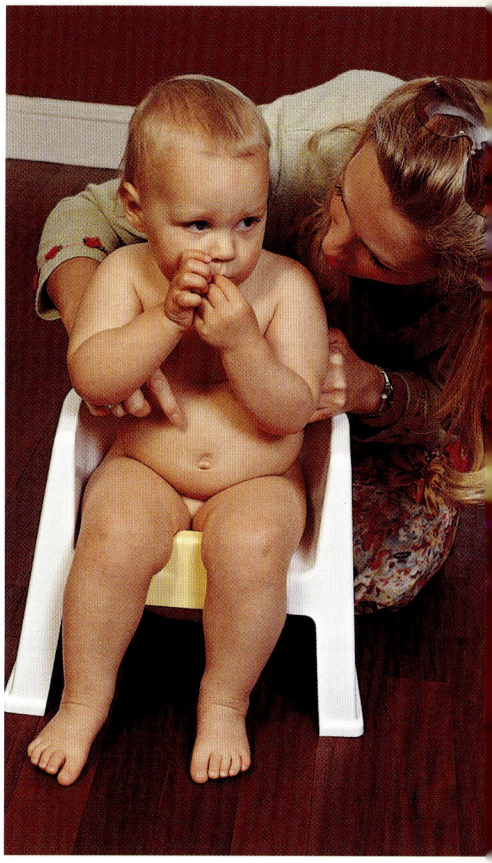

If your child is distressed during potty training, consider all of these – and other – possible contributing factors. Give her specific reassurance about her concern and give her lots of reassurance in general. Hugs and cuddles during potty training help to boost her confidence.

You will find that your child gradually begins to overcome her early anxieties once she grows comfortable with the training routine. Every small success in using the potty pushes her one stage further, as her anxieties diminish and her self-belief grows. You share in her delight with her progress, and she shares in your delight at how well she is doing.

❸ Wetting incidents are punished.

A child does not deliberately wet herself during potty training – these episodes are part of the learning process. Never punish her for those lapses along the way, as they are perfectly normal.

❹ The training becomes hallmarked by stress and pressure.

Both parent and child need to be relaxed while potty training is under way. Fight any feelings of tension you have over potty training.

❺ Parents give up too easily.

A child is disappointed if her parents give up on potty training just because she is making slow progress. So, stick with your support for her, even if training is taking months rather than only weeks.

strategy: Supportive Night Training

The fact that your older child learned bladder control very quickly does not mean that the same will happen with your younger child. Equally, just because your neighbour's child started potty training at this age and yet her child is still not fully trained some months later, does not mean you will experience similar difficulties with your child.

Questions and Answers

My child uses his potty quite happily but he won't sit on the proper toilet in our house. What should I do to encourage him?

The chances are that he is afraid when sitting on the toilet – the normal adult-sized seat can seem huge to a young child. The best solution is to buy a child-sized toilet seat that fits inside your existing toilet seat. This makes him feel steadier and safer when sitting, and he will be altogether more confident on the smaller seat.

Why is it that my toddler sits on the potty without any bother but doesn't use it?

Maybe he is still too young to understand what the potty is for. Since he is happy and cooperative, you could persist with your current approach – he'll get there eventually. Alternatively, you could take a break from potty training until he is a few months older, then start again. The choice is yours.

Every child is unique and this shows through in potty training, too. Studies have also found that in general boys tend to take longer to acquire bladder control than girls (although, of course, this doesn't mean that every single girl is faster than every single boy). Your child will make progress in potty training at his own pace, depending on his mood, enthusiasm, maturity and the level of support you provide for him during what can be a frustrating time for both of you.

Night Training

Your child will almost certainly gain day control before he gains night control. Around 90 per cent of children are dry at night by the age of 5 or 6 years, while the remainder can take another couple of years before achieving a dry bed each night. Most children are ready for night training by the time they reach the age of 3 years. Night training is usually easier than day potty training because by now your child is already used to exercising control over his bowel and bladder muscles during the day.

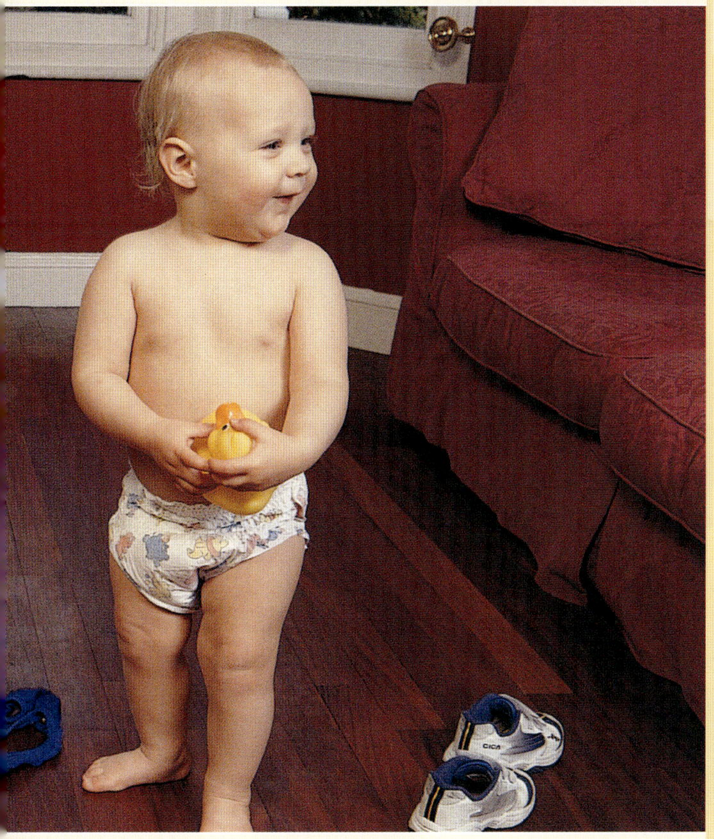

Trainer pants can be useful when your child is getting to grips with using the potty.

When you think he is ready to begin this new stage in his life – perhaps because you find that his night nappy is dry when he wakes in the morning – explain the process to him. Tell him that he can try sleeping through the night without a nappy, and emphasize that he mustn't get upset if his bed is not dry in the morning. As a basic precaution, buy a waterproof cover for the mattress in case he does wet during the night. Show him the route from his bedroom to the toilet on his own, or place his potty in his room. Leave the hall and bathroom lights on at night if that makes him feel more confident.

If you discover that he is dry in the morning, make a big fuss of him – if he is not, reassure him that he will probably be dry the following morning. Persist with your support until he starts to achieve the target. He'll get there in time as long as both of you work together.

5 Practical Principles

1. **Familiarize your child with the potty.**
   Explain to him that he is going to use the potty from now on. Let him play with it and keep it handy. (Some children refuse to use a potty and go straight to the toilet – but they will need a step up and a child's seat.)

2. **Encourage him to sit on it.**
   Take off his nappy after meals – when he is most likely to feel the need to empty his bowels and bladder – and suggest he sits on the potty. He will soon get used to this pattern of behaviour.

3. **Give him plenty of time.**
   Make potty training fun by reading him a story while he sits on it, or by letting him listen to music. He will sit there for longer if there is something to keep him occupied at the same time.

4. **Praise successes.**
   In time, your child will use the potty appropriately, even if unintentionally. Whether planned or accidental, give him lots of praise for this action. This helps to make the whole experience positive for him.

5. **Use trainer pants.**
   As the number of toilet successes increases, think about buying trainer pants for your child. You will need to explain to him the difference between these items and nappies.

strategy: Preventing Bedwetting

It is very likely that night training will go smoothly with your child. However, some children do take longer than others to stop wetting the bed and will need your help in doing so. Surveys have found that around one in five children aged 7 years still wets the bed, as do around one in twenty adolescents. Researchers have also found that parents of a child who wets the bed when she is older often had similar difficulties themselves, which suggests that there may be an inherited dimension.

Types of Bedwetting

Psychologists have identified two types of enuresis (the medical term for bedwetting):

1. **Primary enuresis.** This occurs when a child has never been fully dry at night, even when younger. This could be due to delayed muscular or neurological development; perhaps the child's parents were unable to provide adequate support for her during early attempts at training; or it could be caused by physical problems with her urinary tract. In many instances, the precise cause is not identified.
2. **Secondary enuresis.** This occurs when a child has been reliably dry at night for several months or years and then suddenly starts to wet the bed. The typical cause of this is anxiety – she has an underlying worry that makes her lose bladder control while asleep. For example, she could be concerned about school tests, or perhaps she had an argument with her best friend. She needs help to cope with the anxiety before the bedwetting will stop.

Using a Star Chart

A star chart (see pages 52–53) often works effectively with a child who has primary enuresis. Keep the chart propped up by her bedside, explain it to her and then

Questions and Answers

Our older child is a very deep sleeper. Nothing seems to disturb her once she has nodded off. Could this be the reason she wets the bed?

There is no scientific evidence to prove that bedwetting is linked to deep sleep. On the contrary, a child is most likely to empty her bladder when she moves from deep sleep to shallow sleep. In any case, there is not much you can do to make a child sleep less deeply at night.

Should I use a bell-and-pad device to help train my child at night, as she is 6 years old and still wets the bed regularly?

This is a buzzer device that is designed to wake your child when she begins to wet herself while asleep. It is not suitable for children under the age of 6 years. Also, you might find that your child sleeps through the buzzer, even although all the rest of your family are woken by the noise!

diligently stick on a star for each of her successes. Leave the chart blank if the bed is not dry when she wakes and say something encouraging, such as 'I know you are disappointed but I'm sure you'll have a dry bed tomorrow morning.'

This technique probably works because it concentrates your child's mind on her night-time successes, and because it involves positive reinforcement. If you think a star chart might be effective with your child, try it for a four-week period. Take a break after that if no successes have been achieved in this time.

Whatever the cause of your child's bedwetting, reassure her that it is not something to be worried about.

5 Practical Principles

❶ **Don't rely on night lifting.**
This involves lifting your child from her bed just before you go to bed yourself and taking her to the toilet. The problem with this is that you are taking responsibility for your child's bladder control instead of her doing so herself, and she soon learns to rely entirely on you to wake her for a visit to the toilet.

❷ **Cut down on bedtime drinks.**
While reducing the amount your child drinks before she goes to bed won't solve the problem, it does make sense to reduce her fluid intake at that time. Bear in mind, however, that her bladder will steadily fill at night even without a drink at bedtime.

❸ **Encourage your child to visit the toilet before going to bed.**
Get her into the habit of visiting the toilet as the last thing she does before climbing into bed. She may simply forget to do this, and then be reluctant to get out of bed once she is tucked in warmly under the duvet.

❹ **Stick to original routines.**
It is worthwhile continuing with the technique you first used when night training began – it will work eventually if used patiently, systematically and consistently.

❺ **Don't get angry.**
Despite your frustrations at having to clean yet another wet bed in the morning, there is no point in getting cross with your child. For instance, talk about 'dry' and 'not dry' instead of 'wet'; this helps to create a more optimistic mind-set for her.

Childcare

You should not look on childcare – whether in the form of a playgroup, childminder or nursery – as simply an arrangement to keep your child occupied while you use the time for another activity (typically, to go back to work). Of course, childcare enables you to return to part- or full-time employment, but it also brings huge benefits to your child.

Here are some examples of the benefits of childcare for your child:

- **Her independence increases.** Without you by her side, she learns to become less reliant on you to do everything for her.
- **Social skills improve.** Mixing with a range of other children her own age on a regular basis provides an opportunity for her to develop new social skills.
- **She learns more.** Children learn from each other. Shared games and activities provide new daily learning opportunities.
- **Friendships increase.** Common sense tells you that the more children she mixes with each day, the more friendships she is likely to form. These friendships boost her self-esteem.
- **Her routine is varied.** Instead of following the same routine at home every day, childcare creates welcome variety in her daily pattern of activity.
- **Your relationship becomes more focused.** When you and your child spend time away from each other, you are likely to use time together more effectively.

The most common reason for parents of a child of 2 years or less to use childcare is that it frees them

A good nursery or playgroup can provide excellent pre-school learning for your child.

5 Things to consider about childcare

❶ Personal recommendation.

True, everybody forms their own opinion and what suits one child might not suit another. However, personal recommendation about a particular childminder, nursery or playgroup from someone you know certainly should carry weight and provide you with reassurance.

❷ Qualifications.

Virtually all childcare professionals have the opportunity to undergo proper training in aspects of childcare and child development. Qualifications alone do not guarantee quality provision, but you should think twice before leaving your child with someone who is not sufficiently motivated to seek training.

Once settled, pre-school children enjoy the independence that nursery brings.

to go back to work. Indeed, for many families a return to full-time employment for both parents is a necessity, and this is even more so in a one-parent family. In contrast, the most common reason for parents of a child aged 3 years or older to use childcare is to stimulate his development. Both reasons are fully justified; it all depends on your particular family circumstances.

A Forward Step

Entrusting your much-loved child to the care of someone else is a huge psychological step for you and her, and you'll both need time to adjust. For you, there is a mixture of emotions, ranging from worry to unhappiness or even guilt. For your child, the wrench away from your side can be very disorientating. Try to be positive about it, however. The use of childcare opens up new opportunities and developmental possibilities for everyone in your family, not just her.

Don't expect too much, too soon. You and your child need time to adapt to your new routine. There will probably be teething troubles, minor difficulties and even misunderstandings, which are best sorted out as quickly as possible. Give your child lots of reassurance, speak positively about the people and the other children who are already in the childcare facility, and answer any questions that she poses. After a couple of months, you'll find that everything has fallen into place.

❸ Attitudes.

When placing your child in the temporary care of someone else, it is important to check that you are comfortable with that person's attitude towards children and childcare. Problems can arise where expectations of behaviour vary between home and the childcare establishment. Ideally, there should be harmony.

❹ Standards.

Every place that offers childcare facilities has to meet relevant statutory requirements that safeguard the quality of the provision. Do not be afraid to ask for proof (in the form of certification) that these standards have been met; this is an absolute must.

❺ Convenience.

Remember that your use of childcare facilities has to fit in with your own daily schedule – and you also have to be able to meet the cost. So, make sure that the hours suit you and that if there is a charge this is within your budget. Parents often use a combination of childcare resources for one child.

strategy: Getting Used to Nursery

For most children, the start of nursery involves a combination of excitement (at the prospect of all those new games, toys, activities, adults and children) and anxiety (at the prospect of leaving mum and dad for a few hours). That's why the first day at nursery can be challenging for both of you, as your pre-schooler presses herself against you, refusing to let go of your hand and join in. This reaction is completely normal and there is much you can do as a parent to help your child adjust to this new environment.

Questions and Answers

Our child takes ages to let us go at nursery. Is it okay to stay as long as she wants us to?

Once the first few days are over, make the separation short but reassuring. Establish a routine in which you and your child have a quick kiss and hug, then you hand her to one of the adults there and leave. You can make the separation harder for her if you linger excessively at the start.

Our child cries when we collect her from nursery, as if she doesn't want to come back home. We feel terrible about this. What can we do?

She cries because she has difficulty changing from one situation to another, that's all. The problem can be solved easily by asking the nursery staff to warn your child in advance that you are coming to collect her. If they do this several times in the few minutes before your arrival her tears will turn to excitement.

Any nervousness or anxiety your child displays will almost certainly pass within a couple of days. Of course, some children surge into nursery on their first day without so much as a backward glance at their parent – they brim with confidence and have no anxiety at this temporary separation. Other children react differently, ranging from shyness, to mild fear, to open sobbing. However your child reacts during those early days, give her lots of reassurance. Continually repeat that she will be fine and that you will see her again very soon.

Separation Facts

- A child's anxiety about being away from her parents while at nursery typically declines after a couple of weeks, and usually vanishes altogether after a month at the most.
- There is no connection between tears at separation and later psychological problems – apprehension is a normal reaction to temporary separations.
- Separation anxiety often occurs in a confident child, too – even one who has attended a different nursery before starting at this one.
- Children who experience separation anxiety from their parents when starting at nursery are often more alert, curious and assertive once they settle in.

Helping Her Separate

Consider these strategies for helping your child cope confidently with separation from you at the start of nursery (or any childcare arrangement):

- **Tell her in advance.** Tell your child in advance that she will be going to the nursery (or other carer).

Make sure that she meets the adults and children involved beforehand, so that the situation is not totally new to her.

- **Get her involved.** Your child will settle more easily at the start of each nursery session when she targets a specific activity straight away. Find her something to play with as soon as she arrives.
- **Discuss your return.** You know you are coming back but your child might not realize this. So, make a specific point of telling her: for example, say 'I'll see you very soon, before lunch.'
- **Praise on collection.** Tell her how proud you are that she enjoyed nursery and played with the other children there. She loves you to take an interest and she glows under your obvious approval.

5 Practical Principles

❶ Use a babysitter occasionally.
You use a babysitter for your own benefit but it is good for your growing child, too, as it gets her used to other temporary carers.

❷ Take her to child-centred groups.
A parent-and-toddler group or playgroup will help to build your child's social confidence with others, in your presence.

❸ Enrol your child in an activity class.
Her independence steadily grows through attending a short, structured activity class run by an adult. You can leave the class for a few minutes.

❹ Accept support from friends and relatives.
Leaving your child with friends or relatives while you embark on an activity of your own gives her experience of temporary separations.

❺ Consider using a childminder.
Staying with a childminder even for just an hour a week helps to reduce any potential anxiety at being away from you when she starts nursery.

If there are plenty of interesting activities going on, most children soon lose their inhibitions and join in.

strategy: Tackling Nursery Problem

Although your child will have a great time at nursery, learning new skills, making new friends and interacting with new adults, life rarely goes according to plan – even at this age! Problems can occur and she may need your help to find a solution. Here are some common difficulties children experience at nursery.

Questions and Answers

I have spoken to the staff about my concerns over my child but they don't seem bothered. What else can I do?

Make an appointment to speak in confidence to the person in charge of the nursery, and when you have their complete attention explain your worries. Ask them to identify what the nursery can do to help you resolve your concern. Arrange to meet again three weeks later in order to monitor progress.

My child seems to have so many problems in the nursery. It's one thing after another. Is that normal?

Some children sail through nursery without any complaint while others find life's daily challenges very taxing. Your child is one of those who needs greater than average emotional support and guidance at this stage in her life. Once she feels more secure, she'll take these hurdles in her stride.

Socializing

Nursery staff tell you that although your child has been attending nursery regularly she still doesn't mix well with the other children. She prefers to play on her own, and avoids contact when other children approach. The following strategies may help your child to socialize:

- **Nursery buddy.** Nursery staff can boost your child's social confidence by pairing her with a 'buddy' – an older, more confident nursery child who will ask her to play a game two or three times during each nursery session.
- **Small groups.** Staff can take your child for an activity with a small group of only two or three other children, which she will probably find less intimidating.

Crying

No matter how much reassurance you give her, she walks around the nursery tearfully all day. There doesn't seem to be anything specific troubling her, but she sobs from the moment she arrives to the moment she leaves.

- **Individual attention.** She probably just needs regular and consistent attention to help her settle. One effective approach is to assign one member of the nursery staff to chat to her regularly throughout the session. This extra individual attention makes her feel more secure and increases her sense of belonging. If there is no improvement after a couple of months, consider the possibility that there may be a problem with the nursery itself.

Disliking the Food

Despite the fact that the nursery serves a choice of snacks at breaktime and of meals for lunch, your child stares at the plate without eating a thing. Persuasion by the nursery staff has no effect, yet when she comes home she is obviously hungry. There are two complementary strategies which may help to break the barrier between 'home food' and 'nursery food':

- **Nursery food at home.** Bring small samples of the nursery food home and serve them to your child in her familiar home surroundings.
- **Home food at nursery.** Take small amounts of your food into the nursery for her to eat there.

A child who is not mixing well needs gentle and sympathetic assistance from staff to help her socialize.

Not Using the Toilet

Nursery staff report that she doesn't go to the toilet at the nursery, even when she is obviously uncomfortable with a full bladder. When encouraged to use the toilet there, she shakes her head firmly and continues playing with the other children. Your child's reluctance could stem from shyness – from the presence of so many other children compared to home. Ask nursery staff to try the following to help familiarize her with the set-up:

- **Privacy.** Staff could take her to the toilet while letting her know that no other children will be there. This additional privacy should help to build her confidence until she goes willingly without prompting.

Difficulties in Making Progress

At the end of the first term or so, the nursery staff inform you that your child is slower at learning new concepts than the other children. For instance, she struggles to learn colour names or has difficulties with puzzle toys. If your child has difficulties with any aspect of learning, she will benefit from planned support by nursery staff – and by you – that is targeted to improve her learning skills:

- **Individual programme.** Staff could set aside time daily to work with your child on colour recognition, for example, until she grasps the principles. This approach applies to all aspects of learning.

5 Practical Principles

❶ **Be patient with your child.**
Her problems in nursery might seem small to you but they seem very large to her, so take them seriously. She needs your understanding and support to get through this difficult phase.

❷ **Talk to her.**
The first step in trying to understand why something troubles your child is to ask her. Of course, she might not always be able to give you a direct answer but it is worth a try.

❸ **Consider various solutions.**
There is usually more than one way to solve a problem your child faces. Take some time to reflect on the possibilities before deciding on a course of action.

❹ **Follow solutions through.**
Once you have made a decision about what to do next in order to ease the pressure on your child, follow that through until the problem is solved and your child is happier.

❺ **Review the process.**
She learns from experience, so chat with her about the problem and the solution. This boosts her confidence and reinforces the idea that challenges in life can be overcome.

Readiness for School

Readiness for school is an ongoing process, not a specific point that is reached. In other words, it is never the case that a child is not ready for school one day and then she is ready the next. Your child acquires new skills gradually during the pre-school years and it is the combination of these talents and abilities that suggests she is ready for the challenge of school.

If you have concerns about your child's readiness for school, identify the key areas that worry you: for instance, she doesn't make friends very easily, she can't yet recognize her own name in writing or she has difficulty with instructions. Give her practice in these areas so that she gains competence.

Delaying the start to infant school may be an option but is not one to take lightly, as it will create an artificial age gap between your child and her eventual classmates. You should only use this strategy if you are convinced that a further year at the pre-school stage would result in a significant improvement in her school readiness – if not, send your child to school according to her age.

Useful Pre-School Skills

Here are some skills to practise with your child in the months leading up to the start of school, as they will help prepare her for some of the personal challenges there:

- Taking turns in a game and sharing her toys with her friends.
- Taking off her coat, shoes and socks by herself.
- Following a basic instruction like 'put the book on the shelf'.

Some children start school already familiar with letters and numbers but those who do not catch up fast.

5 Personal qualities for school

❶ Strong motivation.
Your child should look forward to school each day, tackling all assignments with enthusiasm. She makes better progress when her motivation is high – a passive, bored pupil is unlikely to make good learning progress.

❷ Self-belief.
A child who values herself, and who believes in herself and her abilities, approaches new challenges in the classroom with excitement, not apprehension. She is confident enough to run the risk of failure.

Children starting school will need to dress and undress themselves so practise these skills at home.

- Being fully toilet trained during the day and able to dress herself.
- Paying good attention to other children when they speak to her.
- Listening to you when you ask a question and giving you an appropriate answer.
- Staying with a babysitter without creating a fuss when you leave.
- Cooperating with her pals during a joint play activity or game.
- Taking responsibility for her personal hygiene during the day.
- Giving her name, address and date of birth when asked.
- Sitting quietly and sustaining an activity for a few minutes.

Personal Qualities

Some parents think that the best way to help their child get ready for school is by teaching her basic educational skills. After all, you might reason, school is all about learning: a child who starts off knowing the early steps of the three 'Rs' should have a head start. While that is positive, your child's educational gains during her first year are not the main factors that give her a good start at school. Discussions with infant teachers confirm that personal qualities – rather than learning qualities – are the characteristics that matter most in the infant class.

❸ Listening skills.

Most learning involves listening, at least to start with. Your child should be able to pay attention to the teacher when she speaks to her, and to her friends when they discuss topics together as a group in the classroom.

❹ Friendliness.

A child rarely learns alone in the infant class – most assignments involve working in pairs or groups. This means that your child's ability to mix easily with others has a direct influence on the progress she makes.

❺ Self-reliance.

Now that she is in the infant class, your child is expected to manage on her own without seeking adult help at every turn. This includes the ability to settle at a task when instructed to do so, and eating her snack independently.

strategy: Preparing for School

The transition from nursery to school is a huge step for your child and there are many changes for him to manage. Here are some of the common challenges he faces and suggestions for how you can help.

Classroom, School and Playground

Unlike the nursery, the infant class is probably only one small part of a much larger building. The toilets are further away, there are more rooms, wider corridors and lots of stairs to negotiate. Help to reduce your child's apprehension by:

- **Reassurance.** Give your child confidence that he'll be fine – a school building can be an intimidating place for a 5-year-old.
- **Identifying the infant area.** Show him the area set aside for the youngest classes in the school.
- **Familiarization.** Make sure your child has a chance to visit the school and walk around the entire building before he starts there.

Routine

The infant school has a routine that the pupils are expected to follow. This structured pattern of events enables targets to be achieved and helps children plan ahead. However, routines can be demanding for a new pupil so help to prepare your child:

- **Structure at home.** Develop a fixed routine at home in the months prior to him starting school.
- **Involvement in planning.** Ask him to think about his daily routine and suggest ways in which it might be changed.
- **Planning practice.** Teach him to plan ahead. For instance, if you plan a shopping trip for the afternoon, encourage him to prepare his outdoor clothes a few hours before you set out.

Expectations of Pupils

Adult expectations of children are higher at the infant stage than when they are at nursery. It is assumed they will be more independent and less reliant on help to complete tasks. The following strategies will help to get him used to these new experiences:

- **Group work.** When his friends come around to play, give them a simple activity that they have to do together, such as sorting shapes into piles.
- **Less attention.** Cut down on the help you offer your child. When he doesn't know what to do, wait a few seconds before assisting.
- **Self-reliance.** Expect more of your child at home during the months prior to starting school, for tasks such as dressing himself or tidying his room.

Staff and Pupils

There will probably be several hundred pupils in your child's school, most of them older than him. He also has to get used to dealing with a large number of adults, and the following strategies may help him in this:

- **Social opportunities.** Your child's ability to cope socially with the infant school is improved by attending nursery.
- **Meet the teacher.** Take advantage of any opportunity for your child to meet his infant class teacher before starting there. Make sure he realizes that he has to do what the teacher asks.
- **Pecking order.** He is now the youngest in school, not the oldest in nursery. Reassure him that the other pupils are caring and supportive.

Class Curriculum

Although nurseries typically follow a recognized pre-school curriculum, the curriculum of the infant class is more structured and demanding. This can present serious challenges for a young pupil who is used to a less formal approach. Try these strategies:

- **Understanding.** Explain to your child the wide range of activities he is likely to meet in his new school.
- **Different materials.** Show him some of the materials that are found in an infant class, such as a

Encourage your child to complete activities without your help – at school he will need to work independently.

reading scheme and computer equipment with its associated programs.

- **New dimensions.** Point out some of the new activities your child might not yet have experienced, such as physical education or drama.

Questions and Answers

My child gets quite anxious in large, noisy places. How can I prepare him for this aspect of school?

Letting him see around the school during term time will help. You can also take him to large shopping centres, railway stations and other noisy buildings to get him used to the sights and sounds. He will adapt quickly when you are there to reassure him. This preparation builds his confidence and makes him less anxious about the school building.

My child is always the last to get ready. How will he cope with all the changes that take place during the school day?

He'll improve naturally through wanting to keep up with his classmates. Also, give him practice in getting ready more quickly. For instance, time how long it takes him to put a book away or put his shoes on, then make it a game to complete these activities faster.

5 Practical Principles

❶ **Don't leave it all to chance.**
Think about the new challenges facing your child when he starts school, and try to anticipate some of the difficulties he might experience. That's better than simply trusting to luck.

❷ **Have a positive attitude.**
Your enthusiasm for starting school will spread to your child; your optimism feeds his. So always talk positively about school, about the teachers, about the pupils and about the learning activities.

❸ **Remind him of his friendships.**
Starting school is so much easier for a child when he knows that he has friends who will be in the same class. Point this out to him, explaining this means that he will have pals there right from the start.

❹ **Listen to his concerns.**
No matter how well you prepare your child for school, he may have concerns of his own about this new phase in his life. Let him express these to you openly – and then reassure him.

❺ **Share a sibling's experiences.**
If you have an older child who attends the same school, ask her to explain the exciting moments to her younger brother. (Make sure she doesn't regale him with any doom-and-gloom tales.)

strategy: Homework Support

Every school has a homework policy that specifies clear expectations of the amount of work a pupil is to do at home, in order to supplement his classroom curriculum. Homework is not a punishment, it is an additional means of enhancing your child's progress while at the same time providing you with a chance to get involved indirectly with his learning. Try not to let your child's homework become a problem.

Questions and Answers

I feel the school staff pick on my child. What should I do?

They are unlikely to pick on him. More probably, your child has difficulties settling into the class routine. Meet his teacher and listen to what he or she has to say. Be prepared to accept that your child could have such difficulties and work with the teacher to resolve them. Try not to allow barriers to develop between you and school staff.

When I help my child with his homework, I often end up doing it for him. How can I avoid this?

You have to strike a better balance between supporting your child with homework and actually taking over. It's good that you take an interest, but make sure your child remains involved. Offer advice, give possible solutions. Sit with him while he tries out your ideas, but do not do the work for him.

Learning Problems

Every child learns at his own rate and moves through the curriculum at his own pace. If you are aware that your child has learning difficulties – either from your own observations or from school reports – speak to his class teacher. These difficulties may be of a temporary nature (because there is a specific area of the curriculum with which he struggles) or they may be more long lasting (because he has underlying general learning difficulties).

Your main priority should be to ensure that your child receives a programme of work and additional support that meets his learning needs. In your discussion with school staff, check out the following:

- The class teacher's view of your child's particular learning problem.
- For how long the difficulty has been noticed.
- What help the school has already provided for him.
- The modifications made to his learning materials in the classroom.
- What progress your child has made with this help.
- What additional learning support school staff intend to provide next.
- The advisability of seeking further professional assessment.
- The plan for reviewing your child's progress in the future.

Behavioural Problems

Children can present a wide range of behavioural difficulties in the classroom, but most of these can be managed effectively. The most effective way of dealing with behavioural difficulties is usually a combined approach involving school staff and the child's parents. That's why it is best not to react defensively when the class teacher tells you, for instance, that your child shouts out in class, or that he is too quiet, or that he is aggressive with his peers.

A quiet space where your child can do homework without distractions is important.

Listen to what the class teacher tells you, and then discuss ways of resolving the problem. For instance, a child who is aggressive towards his classmates often benefits from a very clear structure of rules, with a system of associated rewards for good behaviour and punishments for aggressive behaviour. When the same techniques are used at home by his parents as well as by school staff, progress tends to be more rapid.

Whatever the problem, talk to your child about it. Let him know that you and the class teacher are working together to help him. Put this to him positively, so that he starts to feel motivated to change, too. Praise any behavioural progress he makes.

5 Practical Principles

1. **Take it seriously.**
   Make completion of homework a priority, so that your child develops a positive attitude towards it.

2. **Suggest a structure.**
   You could advise, say, that he does his homework a few minutes after he comes home, or perhaps immediately after the evening meal.

3. **Make space.**
   Your child completes homework more effectively when he has his own designated space in which to lay out his workbooks and pencils.

4. **Remove distractions.**
   He thinks more clearly when the television is switched off. Siblings should be discouraged from interrupting him during homework.

5. **Offer help.**
   Be prepared to give advice from time to time. He may be genuinely stuck with a particular piece of work – it may not be that he cannot be bothered to do it himself.

Enjoying Hobbies

No matter how busy your child's life is, it's good for him to have a special hobby that particularly fires his interest, such as painting, gymnastics, sports, music or drama. A hobby allows your child to build up specialist skills and knowledge. Many activities involve lessons in a group under adult supervision, and this further improves his ability to listen, concentrate and cooperate.

Here are some points to consider:

- **Pressure.** Remember that you cannot force your child to take up a hobby, although it is helpful to make suggestions and create opportunities. There are many parents who were determined their child would learn to play the piano, only to find that the unplayed instrument stands in the corner gathering dust.
- **Wait before spending.** That's why it is best not to make large financial outlays at the start – wait until your child has been actively involved in the leisure activity of his choice before buying the associated equipment. In the meantime, musical instruments can be rented and sporting equipment borrowed.
- **Assess progress.** If you find your child is no longer making progress in his hobby and his enthusiasm seems to be evaporating, this may be the time to assess whether or not he should continue. You don't want him to give up too quickly, but there is no point in going with an activity just for the sake of it.

Over-organized?

There is a danger that if your child has too many hobbies, attends too many leisure classes and has too

Make sure your child has time to play freely outside if he enjoys this.

5 Ways to keep your child fit

❶ **Encourage him to walk to school at least once a week if possible.**

Walk with him, teaching him road safety. Children under 10 years old have difficulty judging traffic speed.

❷ **Let him run around the local park at the weekends.**

You can sit and watch (if you want) while he runs around playing on the grass with his friends.

A physical hobby like dancing is a great way of getting exercise and helps to improve coordination.

many interests, he may become swamped. The fun goes out of his leisure time.

- **Unable to choose.** You want him to learn and to use his time effectively, but he also needs to be able to make decisions for himself. Too many pre-planned learning activities reduce his ability to make choices.
- **Exhausted.** Too much time devoted to an endless stream of leisure classes that dominate his weekends or weekdays makes him tired, bored and irritable. He needs time to himself.
- **Stressed.** The pressure of meeting targets at each of the different leisure classes can place stress on your young child. The end-of-term drama show or the next music grade exam can be too much for him.

To decide if your child's time is over-organized, ask yourself the following questions:

Does he have time for free play? If you notice that he never seems to have any time to play with his toys, then maybe he is too busy with organized activities.

Is he enthusiastic about his hobby? He should anticipate the leisure activity with at least some spark of interest – think again if his motivation is low. If he doesn't appear to enjoy the activity much, then perhaps he is being pushed too hard.

Is he irritable? A child who is over-organized with too many activities can be complaining and uncooperative. He grows moody and confrontational.

Does he ask to stop going? Repeated comments that he would like to stop the leisure class should be taken seriously.

❸ Encourage a physical hobby.

This could be something like swimming or athletics. There is bound to be some physical activity that he would enjoy in his leisure time.

❹ Go walking or jogging together at the weekend.

Slow your pace to his so that you move together – this also gives you time to talk to each other.

❺ Consider active family holidays.

There are plenty of travel companies that offer walking tours or outdoor activities – this makes a change from beach holidays.

strategy: Alleviating Boredom

There are few comments more likely to make your hackles rise than your bored child telling you 'I don't have anything to do now.' You know he has lots of toys, games and books, half of which he has barely used in the past few months, and therefore his plea of boredom fills you with astonishment. However, a child who is unable to occupy himself can have lots of play equipment all around – what he lacks is the right attitude. He needs to take some responsibility for organizing his leisure time.

If you need to limit your child's television viewing, offer him some interesting alternative activities.

Couch Potato

Perhaps worse than having a bored child hanging around you all day is having a child who sits in front of the television all day. He would happily stay glued to that same spot viewing one programme after another.

You need to set limits on his television time. Don't be afraid to put a specific figure on it, or to identify certain programmes that he is permitted to watch. Of course, he'll complain that he has nothing else to do or argue that there is nothing wrong with watching television all day. Don't give way: place these limits and then stick to them. In between times, keep the television off.

Questions and Answers

My child wants to use the computer only to play games. How can I change his outlook?

Show him that the computer has other potential uses which he might find fun or interesting. For instance, he can use it as a word-processor for preparing homework assignments or topics. He can also use it to play educational games or run informative programs, and can access the web for information resources. Demonstrate these other uses and then get your child involved in them whenever you can.

What should I do with a child who refuses to get up from the couch and do something? He just won't budge and starts to cry when I get annoyed.

Continue to persuade him despite his tears – remember that it is in his best interests, physically and mentally, to have a range of activities. In the beginning, set an easy target – suggest that if he shares an activity with you for, say, 15 minutes, you'll let him return to his couch-based activity.

Another way to break the routine of the couch potato is by making sure he sits around the family table for meals, and does not eat off a tray while glued to the television. Make sure that the television cannot be seen from the table. This helps to break the link between eating and watching television (plus it helps to boost the level of communication between you and your child).

Hooked on Computer Games?

Problem: He plays computer games for hours on end.
Strategy: Reach an agreement with him on the amount of time he can spend playing these games. Monitor this to ensure that he sticks to this regime.

Problem: Your child insists that his friends' parents let them play all day if they want.
Strategy: Let him know that you know it isn't true. If he persists, call his bluff by phoning the parents of one of his friends – that will resolve the discussion quickly.

Problem: He tells you he plays computer games because he has nothing else to do.
Strategy: Chat to him about alternatives, such as drawing, jigsaws, ball games and so on. Suggest he plays at one of these other activities at least once a day.

Problem: Your child reaches for the computer switch the minute he wakes up.
Strategy: Persuade him to have one (or two) days a week without the computer. Let him choose the days in advance, and encourage him to plan other activities.

Problem: The only time your child is settled is when he is playing games on his computer.
Strategy: Sit with him during non-computer activities and encourage him to persist at these for longer before he gives up. His tolerance of these challenges should increase steadily over time.

5 Practical Principles

1. **Suggest he makes a list of every one of his toys, games and books.**
The very act of compiling this list increases his awareness of his possessions.

2. **Help him to plan his day in more detail.**
For instance, he can set aside half-an-hour to 'play with jigsaws' or one hour to 'read books'.

3. **Suggest to him that he limits himself to only two or three different leisure activities in any one weekend day.**
He will focus better when there are fewer choices.

4. **Discuss the range of possible choices with him.**
Your interest makes him more enthusiastic about planning his activities.

5. **Give him lots of encouragement when he does fill his time purposefully.**
Tell him how pleased you are that he organized himself without any prompting from you.

strategy: Taming a Daredevil

Your child loves to explore – that's what makes life so exciting for him. The problem, however, is that he doesn't have a well-developed sense of danger. Of course, he knows that people get hurt and die, but this knowledge doesn't actually mean anything to him at this stage. To him, accidents are things that happen to other people.

As a parent, though, you know the potential pitfalls awaiting your intrepid young explorer, such as falling down the stairs, getting burned when playing with matches or even being knocked down by a car while running across a busy road. The list of possible hazards facing your child is endless. Here are some facts about daredevil behaviour that psychologists have uncovered:

- When he is aged 2 years or under, your child is not good at anticipating danger, so you have to be extra-vigilant at that stage.
- Your child's ability to curb his daredevil behaviour is further reduced when he is highly excited – the surge of adrenalin dulls his sense of danger.
- When a boy is injured through daredevil behaviour he usually blames others, whereas a girl is more likely to blame herself.
- Parents are more likely to put up with reckless, adventurous behaviour from their young son than they are from their young daughter.

Too Cautious

The opposite of the daredevil is the child who is so afraid that he won't try anything new at all. Just as you worry about your impetuous explorer, you would also be concerned if he became so afraid of danger that he wouldn't leave your side. A child with that outlook on life sticks only with what he knows and is used to – he shuns new experiences and misses out. This keeps him safe and sound, yet his quality of life is diminished. Try the following approaches to help build up his confidence without pushing him too hard, too soon:

- **Gentle persuasion.** Most cautious children freeze totally under pressure to be more adventurous, so persuade your child, rather than force him into something he doesn't want to do.
- **Manageable aims.** Set your child targets that are not too challenging: for example, if he refuses to budge past the first rung of the small ladder to the top of the slide, encourage him to go to the second

Questions and Answers

How can I get my daredevil to listen to me? He usually ignores my warnings.

You may get more of a response from him if you tell him why he can't do these things. Pitch your explanations at a level suitable for his understanding. For instance, 'If you play with matches, you will burn your hand and this will be very painful for you' is a better approach than 'Playing with matches is naughty so don't do it'.

I've warned my child so much about danger that now he's afraid to play outside with his pals. What should I do?

You have to strike a sensible balance, one that recognizes that he can never be completely safe but that neither should he take unnecessary risks. Use a well-planned combination of sensible guidelines about keeping safe, coupled with positive advice about how he can have excitement without danger. This will be an effective approach.

step, and then cease that activity for the day while he is ahead and before it goes wrong. He will be pleased with his small success.

- **Encourage him to follow another child.** Take him to the park or playground with a 'bolder' friend or older child. He may be less timid when he sees them in action.
- **Don't make fun.** Never laugh at his timidity. Your child won't see the funny side of your humour or ridicule when it revolves around his fear. He needs to know that you take him seriously.

If your child is likely to experiment with dangers despite warnings, letting him do so under your supervision may dispel his curiosity.

5 Practical Principles

❶ **Set limits on his activities.**
Explain clearly to him that certain objects or areas of the house are out of bounds, and redirect his interest elsewhere.

❷ **Do not overdo warnings about danger.**
Your child might become afraid to try anything new at all, and that is not what you want you to achieve.

❸ **Provide safe experiences.**
Make sure he has plenty of opportunities to explore safely, so that he doesn't need to put himself at risk to achieve adventure.

❹ **Enrol your child at a leisure class.**
These classes are thoroughly supervised, and are designed to stretch his abilities and talents within a safe environment.

❺ **Positively reinforce his sensible behaviour.**
Give him lots of praise when you see him avoid a potential hazard by choosing a safer option.

Sibling Rivalry

Jealousy and tension between children in the same family is so common that most psychologists consider it to be part of normal family life. This does not mean you should simply accept bickering between your children without question, but equally you shouldn't feel you are somehow at fault as a parent just because there is occasional rivalry between them. In any case, there is lots you can do to minimize the effects.

Fights between siblings are normal, but consistent patterns of tension can be reduced if you understand what is causing them.

Sibling rivalry occurs for a number of reasons:

- You have limited time and resources for your children.
- They have different talents, personalities and strengths.
- They have to compete for their share of attention.
- Your children's life achievements differ at every stage.
- Each child's need for your love instinctively fights against possible competitors.

How Rivalry Shows

Jealousy between children will usually show in subtle ways. For instance, one of your children might 'accidentally' knock over her sibling's toys on her way to the kitchen, or perhaps one of your children hurts himself just as you are praising his older sister, so that you have to turn your attention to him instead. You might even find that when your new baby comes home from the hospital, your first-born child starts to wet herself during the day even though she was dry before the baby was born.

In order to understand sibling rivalry, think before you respond to your children's bickering or challenging behaviour. Ask yourself whether the real reason for their dispute is jealousy rather than the apparent reason – for instance, one child claims the other made an annoying comment. If there is a consistent pattern of tension between your children, insecurity stemming from sibling rivalry may be the true cause.

Facts About Sibling Rivalry

- Rivalry tends to be strongest when the youngest child is

Siblings may argue bitterly one moment and play cooperatively the next!

around 3 or 4 years old.

- Fist fights are more common than verbal disagreements when one of the children is around the age of 2 or 3 years.
- When siblings aged 3 or 4 argue with each other, the disagreement usually revolves around a game or toy.
- When brothers and sisters aged 4 or 5 years engage in conflict, they are more concerned with demonstrating their own power.
- Every child is different. One of your children might have no problem with her siblings, while another might be extremely jealous of them.

Age by Stage

1–2 years: Your toddler is very self-centred and doesn't think much about the feelings other people have. Her main interest lies in getting exactly what she wants, when she wants it. This means that sibling rivalry is not very strong because she is too self-focused to be bothered about younger and older siblings.

2–3 years: The typical 2-year-old has a strong sense of self-importance. She assumes the world will revolve around her and has a raging tantrum when she discovers that she may not be the centre of attention. The prospect of a new baby can rock her emotional security, resulting in jealousy of the new arrival. Her older sibling may find her extremely annoying.

3–4 years: At this age your child has her own opinions, likes and dislikes – she doesn't want anyone to interfere with her plans, which is why she may find her younger sibling irritating and threatening. Your attention to him frequently unsettles her. She also resents being bossed around by her older siblings, even though their expectations of her behaviour are reasonable.

4–5 years: Sibling relationships change now. Instead of feeling annoyed by the new baby, your older child is more positive, wanting her young sibling to admire and respect her. She tries to set a good example. In turn, she looks up to her older siblings and acknowledges their achievements, although these may either act as an incentive or, conversely, cause her to resent them.

5–6 years: School changes life for the typical 5-year-old. She now has her own structured world in which there is ample scope for her to make friends outside her family circle. This causes her to be more tolerant of her younger siblings. Older siblings tend to be more highly valued at this age, too, because she can benefit from their experience and guidance on school-related matters.

7–8 years: She is well established in school and has her own set of friendships, which she values highly. Interruptions from younger siblings are typically tolerated less well than before – she regards them as embarrassing when she is with her friends, rather than cute! There may be instances where an 8-year-old asks for specific help from an older brother or sister because she knows they are reliable.

strategy: Meeting the New Baby

Expect your first-born child to be at least slightly troubled when he realizes that there is a new baby on the way. He may be young (typically, aged between 2 and 4 years), but he's smart enough to know that when he is not the only child in the family he will have to share your attention – you just can't give him as much of your time as you did when he was the only child at home.

Your first-born also guesses that you will have less patience with him because you'll be stretched between two children. He will be worried that his routine could be disrupted, as the time you need to give to your baby means he might not be able to continue with his current way of life.

Reassurance

Be ready to give your first-born child lots of reassurance when you tell him about the new baby. Here are some of his potential anxieties:

- You will love the new baby more than you love him.
- The new baby will take all of your attention away from him.
- You want a new baby because he has done something wrong.
- The new baby won't love him.
- He will have to move out of his bed to make room for the baby.
- He won't be able to continue attending playgroup or nursery.

These fears may seem ridiculous to you but they are very real to an anxious 3-year-old, who would rather that life continued the way it is than change because of another child in the family. Be patient with your first-born – he needs time to adjust.

Let your child touch and talk to the new baby as this will help him to feel that he is involved and has something to offer.

The First Meeting

Plan and prepare for the first time your older child meets his new sibling, which will probably be in the maternity hospital the evening after the delivery. These strategies will help the meeting to go smoothly:

- **Go with the flow.** Your first-born may be distant and aloof, clinging tightly to your partner instead of rushing over to you. He is just a bit overwhelmed by it all. Relax – he'll unwind within a few minutes.
- **Talk to him.** Make your first-born child the total focus of your attention in those early minutes. Ask about his activities since you last saw him. You'll find he gradually drifts towards his new sibling.
- **Swap presents.** Tell your child that the baby has a gift for him in his cot (one you brought with you to the hospital) and quietly give him a present to give to the baby. This may be contrived, but it usually works.

Questions and Answers

Since my baby was born two months ago, our 4-year-old has started sucking his thumb and using baby talk. Why does he do this?

This return to an earlier stage of development (known as 'regression') is a common response to stress during childhood. Anxiety over the new baby has caused him to act at an earlier stage of development, which he associates with more attention from you and less psychological pressure. He'll pass through this phase.

Should I let our 3-year-old touch the baby? He is jealous of her and I'm afraid he might be rough.

Loving physical contact (stroking and cuddling) is a great way to strengthen the bond between child and baby, and therefore this should be encouraged. You have nothing to worry about as long as you are there to supervise and intercede should your child be too enthusiastic physically with his little sister.

5 Practical Principles

❶ **Explain about the baby early on.**
The best time to explain about the baby is when your 'bump' begins to show, usually around when you are five or six months pregnant.

❷ **Match explanations to his understanding.**
Don't go into too much detail. Children aged 3 or 4 years do not require an in-depth explanation of events.

❸ **Talk positively.**
Look excited when you tell your first-born about the new baby, even though you are probably worried about his reaction.

❹ **Answer his questions.**
Once the news has sunk in, your child will want to ask you lots of questions. Give honest, reassuring answers.

❺ **Let him explain to others.**
Give your child the opportunity to tell visiting friends and relatives about your news (even though you have probably told them already).

strategy: Reducing Sibling Bickerin

Fights between children in the same family are an everyday occurrence. You cannot have more than one child under the same roof without moments of tensions arising, but there is lots you can do to ease those difficulties and prevent them escalating into major disagreements.

Completing a task together is a great way of getting children to cooperate, as long as each feels he has been given equal responsibility.

The Age Gap

Research confirms that the effects of sibling rivalry depend to some extent on the age gap between your children. This is probably because children who are closer in age tend to feel more competitive towards each other (even as they grow older) than those between whom there is a large age gap.

- **Age gap of less than 18 months:** sibling rivalry is generally less intense. When children are born so close together, jealousy is reduced.
- **Age gap of two to four years:** sibling rivalry tends to be very high. Ironically, this is the most common age gap between a first and second born child.
- **Age gap of more than four years:** rivalry is less intense once again. Sibling relationships tend to be more positive with a larger age gap.

Why it Matters

The peak level of jealousy at an age gap of two to four years arises for several reasons:

- The older child has a well-organized life that he wants to continue as before.
- He knows that the baby will make demands on you and that he will need to wait while you are busy.
- He is so used to having you to himself that he can't imagine what an extended family will be like.

Compare this with an older child who has already spent a considerable amount of time outside the family home away from his parents, perhaps at nursery or pre-school, or just playing with his friends. He is more confident and less vulnerable to the effects of change. A toddler younger than 18 months won't notice the new arrival much, either. Remember, however, that these research findings are only general trends – your own children may respond differently.

In addition, the effect can change as the children themselves grow older. For instance, you may find your 3- and 4-year-olds fight constantly, but become best friends by the time they reach secondary school age.

Questions and Answers

What is the ideal age gap between a first and second child?

There is no 'ideal' that suits every family. It all depends on your personal circumstances. Some parents prefer to wait until their first child is well established in nursery before thinking about having another child, while other parents want to have their children spaced closely together in the hope that they will be good friends. It really is up to you to decide what best suits you and your family.

Our older child is talented. Our younger one strives to be like him but he is less able. What should we do?

Children often generate comparisons with siblings, even when parents avoid this. A useful strategy would be to encourage your younger child to develop his own interests, his own hobbies and his own friends. In other words, emphasize and maximize his uniqueness, as this will boost his self-esteem and make sibling comparisons less relevant to him.

5 Practical Principles

1. **Ignore minor fights.**
Give your children a chance to sort out their disagreements on their own. Try not to jump in too soon when their arguments are petty – otherwise you run the risk of rewarding their fights with your attention.

2. **Teach conflict resolution.**
When you do intervene, help them sort out their disagreement. Sit them facing each other, and ask each in turn to give their account of what happened while the other listens. After this, summarize the problem yourself and ask them to think of ways it can be resolved. Give helpful suggestions if necessary.

3. **Make physical violence unacceptable.**
Set a clear rule that hitting each other is not permissible. They do not have the right to raise their hands to each other under any circumstances.

4. **Treat each child as an individual.**
Each of your children is special, with his own unique blends of characteristics. He wants to feel recognized and valued for the wonderful child he is, not how well he matches up to his siblings. Comparisons are counterproductive and divisive. Statements like 'Your older brother is tidier than you,' simply increase rivalry rather than decreasing it.

5. **Encourage cooperation.**
Give them a joint task to complete, such as putting cutlery on the table for the evening meal or sorting all the toys back into the cupboard. You may have to supervise until the job is done properly.

Practical Problems

AGE 1–2 YEARS

Frustration

Frustration becomes a dominant emotion at this age. Your toddler wants to do so much and his sense of annoyance increases very quickly when things don't go according to plan. In addition, he struggles to control this rapid surge in frustration, resulting in frequent outbursts that are often quite unexpected.

Your Aim

To encourage your toddler to manage his frustration, so that he continues with the task at hand until he achieves his target.

AGE 2–3 YEARS

Misbehaviour at Mealtimes

Eating often becomes more of a game than anything to do with satisfying hunger. This means that mealtimes often prove frustrating for you, as your 2-year-old pushes his food aimlessly around the plate without actually eating it. Alternatively, he may insist on eating only the same specific foods every day.

Your Aim

To establish a settled atmosphere at mealtimes, one which is free from confrontation and tension.

AGE 3–4 YEARS

Fighting

Your child now spends more time playing with other children his own age – this is the only way he can develop social skills. However, fights are common among children of this age and what was a pleasant afternoon can transform almost instantly into a screaming match as your child lashes out at his friend.

Your Aim

To teach your child the appropriate social skills of sharing, taking turns and following rules, which he can then use with his friends.

Helpful Strategies

Do not reprimand your toddler when his frustration spills over. Your own frustration at his reaction makes him even more distressed.

Try to calm him. Wipe away his tears, soothe him with reassuring words and encourage him to continue with the task that is troubling him.

Be ready to offer your child ideas. Frustration often arises because he cannot see a possible solution to a problem.

Distract him from the source of his irritation. Do this for a few minutes when frustration levels are too high, then return to it later.

Helpful Strategies

Accept that you cannot force your child to eat. He will only eat the food in front of him when he makes his own decision to do so.

Stop worrying about his food intake. If your family doctor assures you that your child's weight is within healthy limits, do not make an issue out of eating and mealtimes.

Make mealtimes pleasant occasions. Use this as a time for chatting, as well as eating.

Quietly remove your child's plate even if he has eaten only a little of it. Don't criticize him – he will eat when he is ready.

Helpful Strategies

Help your child practise sharing at home. Encourage him to share his sweets with his siblings and let them play with his toys. Play games with him that involve taking turns as this will encourage him to play more sociably with his pals.

Resolve disputes. Try to calm the situation when he fights with his friend and encourage them to play together again.

Tell your child in advance what will happen if he is hostile towards his friend. Now is the time to take punishment seriously, but also remember that your child responds well to praise for good behaviour.

Explain to your child the practical effects of his aggressive behaviour. Tell him for example, that other children will not want to play with him.

AGE 4–5 YEARS

Sibling Rivalry

Jealousy between brothers and sisters is often strong at this age, because usually both children are old enough to assert themselves. Now, your older child rages at your younger one because she is annoyed by her immature behaviour, while your younger child is annoyed because the older one doesn't give her enough attention.

Your Aim

To encourage your older child to become more tolerant and caring towards her younger sibling, instead of bickering with her all the time.

AGE 5–6 YEARS

Reckless Behaviour

The surge in your child's confidence now that she can do more for herself means that she may be full of herself and almost too confident. She starts to show off in front of her friends or tries to prove to them that she is fearless. What starts out as fun can have serious repercussions.

Your Aim

To maintain your child's self-confidence while reducing her tendency towards reckless behaviour.

AGE 6–7 YEARS

Moaning About School

Now that your child is at school full time, you may find that her enthusiasm for school-based activities is less than you had hoped. Instead of enthusiasm and vigour, you may be faced with daily complaints, moans and groans. In addition, homework just doesn't hold her interest.

Your Aim

To remove possible barriers to your child's motivation for school and boost her confidence in the classroom.

AGE 7–8 YEARS

Disinterest in Family Outings

Your child no longer enjoys family outings. She complains they are dull and uninteresting, and that she would rather be with friends. When you insist that she comes along, she is moody and uncooperative. No matter how much you try, she ends up making everyone miserable.

Your Aim

To encourage your child to feel more connected with other members of the family and to realize that she does have a commitment to them at all times.

Helpful Strategies

Point out the positive qualities of her younger sibling. This avoids her focusing on the negatives all the time. Use her care and concern for her little sister to discourage misbehaviour towards her.

Give your children joint tasks to complete together. Setting the cutlery on the table, for example, encourages them to work cooperatively.

Assign a specific caring task to your older child. This might be reading a story to her younger sibling at bedtime. The thought that others admire her for behaving like a 'big girl' is a reward in itself for good behaviour.

Intervene when your children fight. Settle them and ask each to consider their sibling's position.

Helpful Strategies

Encourage your child's independence. Let her know you are pleased that she is less reliant on you in everyday matters.

Point out her strengths. Explain that her friends like her for who she is, not what she does. She should be herself rather than trying to impress.

Explain basic safety rules. For instance, she should look while crossing the road, she shouldn't climb too high and she should avoid unnecessary risks.

Suggest to your child that she thinks before she does something. Add that she should never do anything hazardous simply to impress her friends.

Helpful Strategies

Take your child seriously. Listen to her complaints and try to determine if she has a specific concern about school.

Talk to her class teacher. The teacher will be able to give you an accurate picture of her current behaviour in school.

Examine her school work closely. This will help you decide whether or not you think she may have a learning difficulty that is affecting her enthusiasm.

Give praise and recognition for her achievements. Let her know you are pleased when she finishes a reading book or brings home a positive message from her teacher.

Helpful Strategies

Involve your child in decisions about family outings. This will give her the opportunity to help choose the focus of the activity.

Make explicit the start and finish times of proposed family outings. Do your best to stick to these times if possible.

Subtly give her some extra attention during the trip. However, avoid asking her repeatedly if she is enjoying herself.

Make a specific point of acknowledging her company. Tell her how pleased you are that she came along when you return home afterwards.

emotional life

4 emotional life

- your child's emotional needs
- emotions and behaviour
- body language
- terrible twos
- managing tantrums
- responding to a rage
- fears and phobias
- spotting signs of fear
- managing fears
- optimist or pessimist?
- reacting to a 'show-off'
- dealing with a bossy child
- fear of failure
- comforting a cry baby
- giving up a comforter
- born to learn
- aiding concentration
- encouraging listening
- emotional problems

Your Child's Emotional Needs

No matter what your child is like, he has emotional needs that drive much of his behaviour. For instance, at a simple level, your child's need to feel loved makes him seek cuddles and reassurances from you; at a deeper level, his need to feel valued causes him to parade his achievements in front of others.

The challenge facing you is to understand your child's emotional needs – when they are met, he is settled and contented; when they are not met, his behaviour can be troublesome and distressing. For example, research shows that children who have still not formed a close loving relationship with at least one caring adult by the age of 3 or 4 years (so that their emotional need to be loved is not met) are likely to have relationship difficulties throughout their lives. Your child's behaviour makes sense when you understand his emotional needs.

Identifying Needs

Here are some of your child's basic emotional needs:

- **To be loved.** We are social animals. We depend greatly on social relationships, the most fundamental of which is the important bond between a child and his parent(s) or carer(s). Your child needs to be and feel loved.
- **To be valued.** He thrives knowing that you think he is terrific. He wants you to be pleased with his achievements and also to value him just for being himself. Your praise and attention makes him feel good.

Your interest in your child's activities and pride in her achievements let her know she is valued and loved.

5 Top Tips

❶ Let him make choices.
Allowing your child to make even minor choices in his life (for instance, what clothes to wear today or what snack to have this afternoon) serves to confirm your trust in him.

❷ Give loving physical contact.
Gentle, warm, loving touch is a fundamental way of showing your love for your child. If he is not keen on this form of contact, he'll let you know.

What an upset child often needs most is to be reassured by close physical contact.

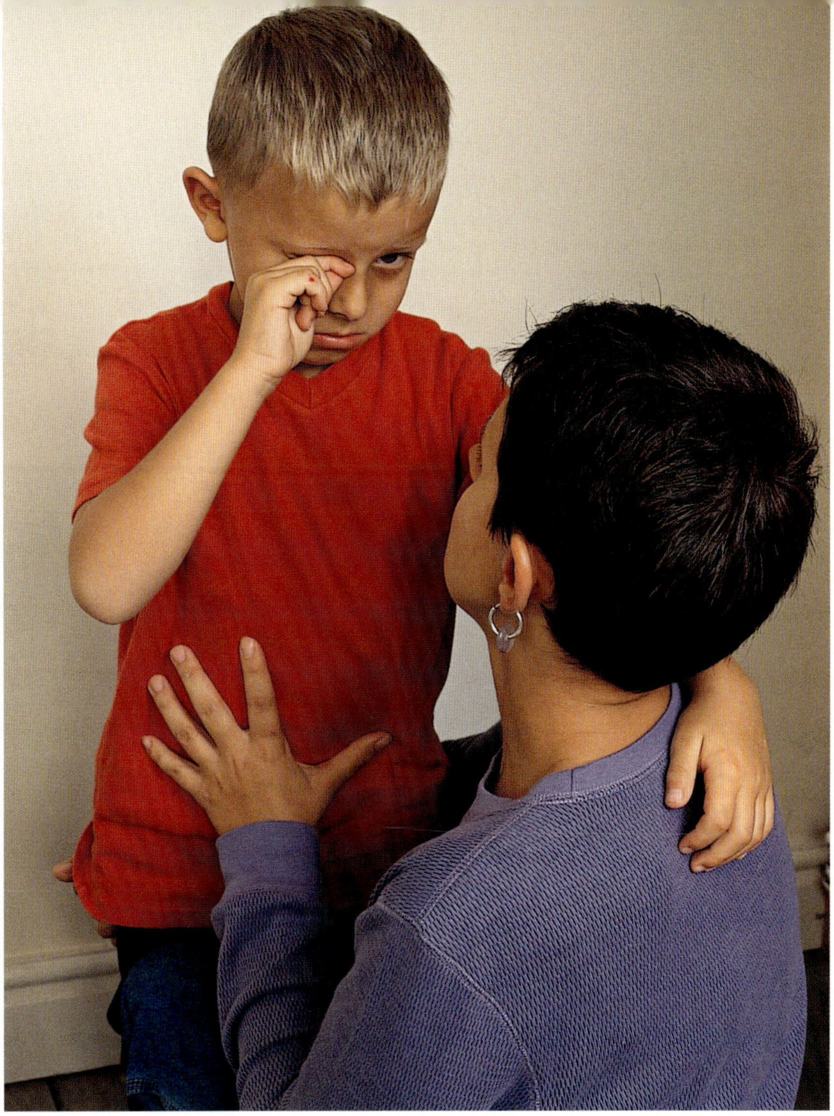

- **To be safe.** A child without a sense of personal safety becomes unsettled and anxious. He needs to know that no harm will befall him and that he can go from one day to the next without fear.
- **To have stability.** Your child requires structure and stability in his life. A predictable routine, with clear boundaries and rules regarding his behaviour, satisfies this need.
- **To feel competent.** It's important for your child to feel capable and that he is able to master the challenges that confront him in day-to-day life. Belief in his own competence enhances his progress.
- **To achieve his potential.** Part of development involves your child expressing his talents and abilities so he can achieve his full potential. This particular emotional need encourages him to try new experiences.

Barriers

Although every child shares the same basic emotional needs, the way these needs are met will vary from child to child, depending on his individual personality and circumstances. For example, your child might be one of those who likes public praise when he makes an achievement – such as praise from family friends on passing a class test – or he might prefer more private acknowledgement of his progress – such as a quiet word of praise from you or even just an extra-special hug.

Think about your child, and his particular likes and dislikes. Find ways to meet his emotional needs that suit his individuality. Do not assume that because his older siblings like you to respond to them in certain ways that the same applies to this one – your children are all different from each other, even though they are being raised together by the same parents in the same household.

❸ Develop a routine.
Your child will thrive emotionally when he is able to anticipate the key events in his daily routine, although you do not need to have a rigid, inflexible routine for every day – this would restrict all spontaneity.

❹ Provide varied opportunities.
The best way to discover your child's true potential is to provide him with a wide range of learning and leisure experiences. He'll begin to home in on the ones he prefers.

❺ Demonstrate that you value him.
Make a big fuss of all his achievements, from his first independent step to a painting he did which he proudly brings home from nursery.

Emotions and Behaviour

Emotions and behaviour are intertwined. Assume that nothing your child does is by chance. Sometimes the link is clear – you didn't buy him a new toy so he had a tantrum. In other instances the link is less obvious – you noticed he was unmotivated about school and eventually found he had fallen out with a classmate. Look for the emotions behind the behaviour.

This link is not always consistent or predictable. Take laughter and fear as an example. Your child grins when amused and trembles when afraid. Sometimes when you reprimand him and make him anxious, he smiles nervously – in this instance, his smile signifies fear of your disapproval, not amusement at your reprimand. Likewise, he can tremble with excitement – for instance, while waiting to go on a ride at an amusement park.

Take Changes Seriously

In the same way that emotions underlie behaviour, the chances are that a change in your child's

5 Top Tips

❶ Encourage regular dialogue with your child.

If he is used to talking to you about his feelings in general, he will be far more open about confiding in you when something troubles him.

❷ Don't expect too much.

Ask your child why he acts in a certain way, but don't expect him to be able to give you a full answer. He is unlikely to be aware of the full range of emotions that influence his behaviour.

behaviour represents a change in his emotions. What matters is the change rather than the specific behaviour itself, whether it is the fact that your child was previously shy and is now totally outgoing or that he was passive and is now aggressive. Changes in behaviour merit close attention, especially when this shift is negative. (Of course, if changes are positive, you'll probably be delighted and not analyse the reasons too much.)

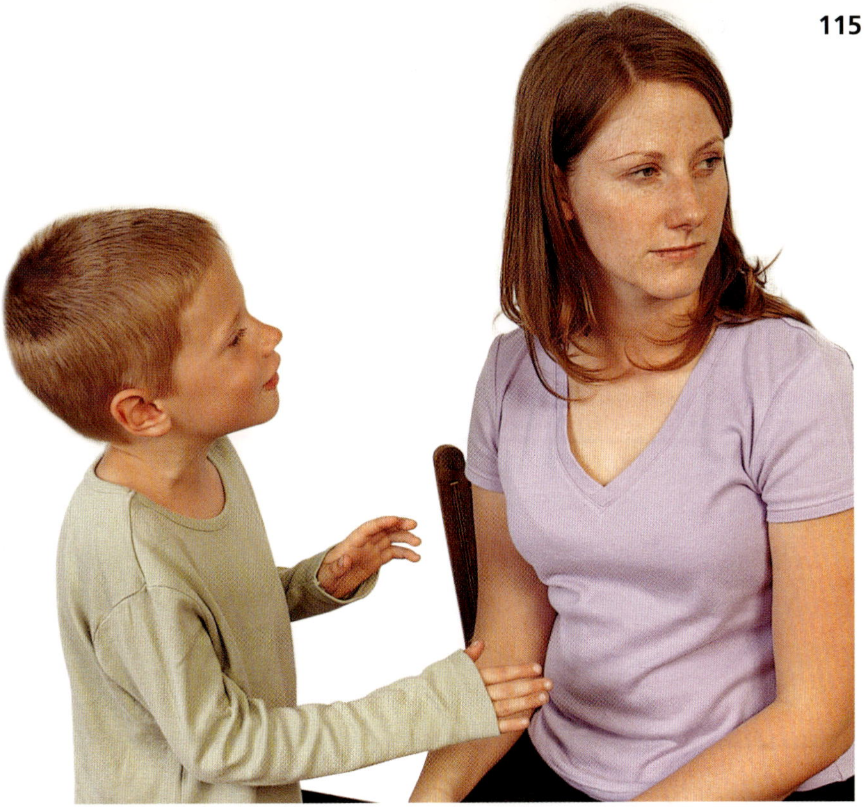

Whenever your child's behaviour alters significantly, ask yourself the following questions:

- What emotions could be driving this change in his behaviour?
- Are there any areas in which he has been experiencing stress?
- Are there any other signs that he is troubled?
- What distressed him the last time he behaved this way?
- Is he aware of the recent changes in his actions?
- What explanation does he give for his behaviour?

Think carefully about the answers to these questions, then use the information you have gathered to help your child resolve the tension or difficulty he is dealing with right now. His behaviour will probably return to its previous nature when the current crisis is resolved.

Laughter usually signals happiness and excitement but can also be caused by nervousness.

School-age children may become more assertive and demanding as they gain independence.

Behaviour or Emotions First?

Once you have established a link between your child's behaviour and his emotions – for instance, that he is more irritable than before the arrival of a new baby – consider how to bring about positive change. You may be uncertain whether to concentrate first on modifying his behaviour (perhaps by encouraging him to be more tolerant) or on changing his emotions (perhaps by giving him lots of reassurance). In fact, the most effective approach is to change both at the same time.

Concentrating on either emotions or behaviour alone does not have as much impact as focusing on both together. Set clear behavioural targets for your child: say, that he should sit at the next family meal without snapping angrily at anyone. At the same time, try to tackle the emotional concerns, perhaps by encouraging him to talk about the issue that you think concerns him.

❸ Consider the obvious, too.

The explanation for a child's actions can be straightforward – for instance, he steals because he doesn't have pocket money. Avoid looking for a complicated explanation.

❹ Expect phases of behaviour.

Changes in behaviour can be linked to wider developmental phases. The pre-school drive towards independence, for instance, often causes a child to become more assertive.

❺ Reflect before reacting.

Don't jump to hasty conclusions. Think about all aspects of your child's life that could be putting him under pressure, including home life, school work and his friendships.

Body Language

Your child does not only express his feelings through spoken language and behaviour – he also communicates his deeper emotions through body language. This form of non-verbal communication – which consists of very subtle, involuntary body movements – is another key to understanding your child's thoughts, ideas, attitudes and feelings.

Body language consists of many different dimensions, including:

- **Facial expression.** Your child tells you he is happy by smiling or that he is miserable by scowling.
- **Eye movements.** You know he is excited because his eyes are bright, wide open and staring into yours; his shifting eye contact tells you he is nervous.
- **Breathing.** When your child is relaxed, his breathing is long and slow; anger makes his breathing shallow and rapid.
- **Personal space.** Cuddling up to you probably indicates that he wants comfort and reassurance, while sitting far away might mean he is annoyed with you.
- **Hand and arm movements.** He crosses his arms defiantly when he argues with you, yet his hands rest by his sides when he feels relaxed and comfortable.

A child's stance and expression are an instant indicator of whether he is sad, angry or upset and may reveal much more than his words.

5 Top Tips

❶ Reflect on body language.
You already interpret much of his body language without making a conscious effort. When you pause to think about this, you can probably compile a list of his gestures that tell you what he feels. For instance, he pulls at his ear when he is tired and he scratches his cheek when he tells a lie. You have made a start already.

❷ Test your interpretations.
A good way to boost your confidence with understanding body language is to interpret a couple of your child's gestures. Once you have done this, ask him what he is thinking or feeling at that moment. His response enables you to match your interpretation with his account. You are probably better at this than you thought.

Why Body Language Matters

There are several reasons why body language is important in your relationship with your child.

- He has less control over his non-verbal communication than he does over spoken language and it is therefore often more revealing than his words or overt behaviour are.
- He uses body language all the time (just as you do) – so it is a useful means of gaining a better understanding of your child.
- When your child is upset or troubled, his spoken communication probably diminishes significantly but his body language persists.
- You may be surprised to learn that around 90 per cent of all emotions are expressed through body language. So, if you cannot understand your child's non-verbal communication then many of his genuine feelings may slip by you unnoticed.

Body language, therefore, is an important souce of information about your child's thoughts and feelings, and the more you can understand it the better. Getting to know the meaning of his non-verbal communications should be high on your agenda.

Start by paying attention to his range of facial expressions – this is the easiest form of body language to interpret – and then start to work out the other, more complex, aspects such as posture and breathing. You will be surprised how quickly you tune into the meaning of his gestures. And the more you do this accurately, the closer you and your child become to each other.

When your child cuddles up to you she is obviously asking for the reassurance of physical contact.

Baby 'Body Language'

Before your baby uses words, his main form of communication is through his crying and facial expressions. You gradually get to know which cry means he is hungry, which one means he is tired and which one means he is bored. This understanding enables you to respond appropriately to him, which in turn strengthens the emotional bond between you. Crying is an important part of body language, especially during his first year.

❸ Mirror his gestures.

Sometimes it is hard to know what a group of body gestures means. To gain clarity, use these gestures yourself and then think about what you feel like when you do so. This 'mirroring' of your child's body language provides you with insight into his inner world and helps you understand what his emotions are at that time.

❹ Be aware of changes.

Your child's non-verbal communication usually changes over time – for instance, the gestures he used as a toddler are likely to be more obvious than those he uses when he has reached school age. That's why you have to stay in tune with him so that you are always sensitive to the changing meaning of his body language.

❺ Accept your limitations.

There are limits to the extent to which you will be able to interpret your child's body language accurately. After all, psychologists claim that there are thousands of different non-verbal gestures that convey meaning! Do what you can, but accept that there are limits.

Terrible Twos

The period between a child's second and third birthdays is often known as the 'terrible twos', because there is typically a marked deterioration in their behaviour. A previously cooperative and even-tempered child can become volatile, hot-tempered and moody whenever she doesn't get her own way.

It is extremely easy to become locked into confrontations with your child because of her self-centred behaviour. In a matter of seconds, a peaceful, relaxing afternoon at home can be transformed into a screaming battlefield as you and your toddler engage in furious arguments – her temper is often triggered by something very trivial. With this pattern of behaviour, you quickly understand where the phrase 'terrible twos' came from.

You need to remember that challenging behaviour at this age is built on frustration, not malice, and that it stems from your child's egocentricity, not her selfishness. Think about this for a moment. Your 2-year-old is egocentric in the true sense of the word: that is, she sees the world only from her point of view. She wants everything her way, and she explodes in anger when this does not happen.

However, she is not selfish in the true sense of the word – she cares deeply about you and she hates it when you are upset, but her egocentricity forces her to put herself first. Over the next year, your child starts to see the points of view of other people. In the meantime, though, it is her way or else!

To an adult a toddler's reaction may seem disproportionate to the cause but her sense of frustration is real.

5 Tantrum triggers

❶ Your insistence that she stops playing and starts to tidy her toys.
This causes her to explode with rage – one minute she is happy, the next she is absolutely furious.

❷ She struggles to fit a piece of her jigsaw into the right place.
Your child's frustration intensifies so quickly in this situation that she loses her temper.

If mealtimes are difficult, try to find ways of taking the attention and pressure off your child.

Terrible or Terrific?

Of course, you have to deal with her tantrums, but there are other ways of making this period in your child's life more terrific than terrible. Most importantly, remind yourself of all the other exciting changes that are going on in her young life at the same time, as this helps you to maintain a balanced perspective on parenting. Positive psychological changes that you can make use of during this period include:

- **Inquisitiveness.** Her knowledge-thirsty mind knows no bounds. Your toddler is desperate to learn about the world around her. You can have great fun helping her make new discoveries with her toys and games.
- **Communication.** Now that her speech and language skills have increased, you can actually have a good chat with her. She likes you to read stories to her, and she asks you lots of questions. The communication between you is much better.
- **Self-sufficiency.** Your toddler does a lot more for herself. For instance, she is probably toilet-trained during the day, and she feeds herself at mealtimes. This means you have a little more time for yourself.
- **Laughter.** A 2-year-old's humour is less mature than an adult's, but you can still have great fun laughing with her. She takes the initiative when trying to make you laugh and she giggles at your humour, too.
- **Relationships.** Other children are more important to your toddler now. She wants to spend more time with them, which eases the intensity of her relationship with you. You can help her sort out any squabbles with her friends.

Facts About Tantrums

- The peak age for tantrums is between the ages of 1 and 3 years, although they can also occur in older children up to the age of 7 or 8.
- There is no gender difference in the frequency of tantrums: girls have just as many as boys, but girls tend to express their anger verbally and boys physically.
- Letting a child do what she wants does not stop tantrums. In many instances, that approach actually increases the number of tantrums as she will learn that she will get her own way.
- Children can be aggressive during tantrums, often hitting out at any innocent victim who happens to be within their range.

❸ You refuse her a bar of chocolate at the supermarket checkout queue.

Your child instantly fills with anger because you won't let her have the sweets she wants.

❹ Her friend won't play the game she wants.

Your child is unable to tolerate this and so she simply loses her temper.

❺ She realizes that you mean what you say.

Although you have told her, say, to stay away from the kitchen while you are cooking, your child explodes with rage when she finally grasps that you are insisting, despite her resistance.

strategy: Managing Tantrums

No matter how good-natured your child and how well she responds to your discipline, there will be times when she loses her temper and explodes into a tantrum. This is normal childhood behaviour so it shouldn't be a cause for concern. However, the more you understand the nature of her outbursts, the better placed you are to resolve them quickly – or better still, to prevent them happening in the first place.

Questions and Answers

Should I talk to my child when she is in a tantrum or should I just leave her until she calms herself?

It depends on your child. In general, however, talking calmly to a child during a tantrum can be very helpful in encouraging her to regain control over herself. This lets her know that you are there for her. If you leave your child alone, the tantrum may run on for longer than is actually necessarily.

Why is it that after a tantrum my child promises to control her temper and yet she can fly off the handle again a few minutes later?

Her promise to behave is genuine – she really does mean this when she makes his pledge. However, she is not yet mature enough to control her temper fully, so she explodes in her usual manner. Do not be dismayed by this, though. You'll find that her tantrums eventually start to diminish in intensity and frequency, with your support and encouragement.

Here are some suggestions for managing your child's tantrums. These techniques will not work every time she has a tantrum, but they do provide you with a starting point:

- **Keep your temper.** Once your child is in a tantrum she has lost all control, so shouting at her won't have any impact. All that happens is that you both end up even more agitated. Force yourself to stay calm when she rages.
- **Maintain perspective.** Of course her tantrums wear you down, but remind yourself that this is a normal developmental phase that she will grow out of eventually. All toddlers have tantrums sometimes, not only yours.
- **Don't be embarrassed.** Your child's displays of rage can be very embarrassing when they occur in full view of the public – in a shopping centre, for example – but you can be sure that most of the onlookers are sympathetic, not judgemental.
- **Avoid where possible.** If you know there are particular situations in which your child's tantrums are more likely for instance, when she plays with her older sister – provide additional supervision at these times, if possible.
- **Look for early warning signals.** Although tantrums can occur in an instant, there are probably warning signs – for instance, her breathing becomes shallower and more rapid. When you see her beginning to get agitated, try to calm her before she reaches boiling point.
- **Distract her attention.** You'll be surprised at how easily your child can be brought out of a tantrum through the simple strategy of distraction. A particular toy or a special video may grab her attention long enough for her to let the tantrum subside.

Sometimes it is possible to step in and lend a hand before your child loses control completely.

- **Do not give in.** Resist all temptation to give in to your screaming pre-schooler for the sake of a quiet life. That approach simply teaches her that she will eventually get her own way if she has a loud enough tantrum. Draw the line of what you will accept and don't let her cross it.

5 Practical Principles

1 Focus on the good times.
At the end of the day, reflect on the happy, shared moments you and your 2-year-old had together. Don't ponder too long on the battles and tantrums that punctuated the day.

2 Break the routine.
Instead of slogging your way through the endless childcare chores and challenges associated with looking after a toddler, plan something special for the two of you, even if she was in a foul mood earlier on.

3 Play with her.
After a draining few hours spent with your bad-tempered 2-year-old, you probably don't feel like trying to relax with her – but do it anyway. Always play with your child for part of the day, irrespective of what her behaviour has been like.

4 Read her a bedtime story.
Your toddler's memory is short. By bedtime, she has forgotten any arguments you had earlier and reading her a story is a good way for you both to mesh again with each other.

5 Share with your partner.
If you have a partner, share your feelings with them. You don't have to pretend that you and your toddler had a wonderful time every minute of the day. You'll feel better after 'sounding off' to someone else.

strategy: Responding to a Rage

Although most tantrums involve a loud outburst of screaming and raging, often with legs and arms flailing about as the child lies angrily on the floor, some children have a breath-holding tantrum. Unlike the typical tantrum that is challenging and forceful, a breath-holding tantrum is quiet and passive. Other children will bite when they are in a rage. Being prepared for this sort of extreme behaviour will help you deal with it when it happens.

During this distressing form of childhood rage, the pre-schooler suddenly and unpredictably starts to hold her breath, often until she loses consciousness. Her anger becomes so strong that she sucks in her breath, blocking the back of her throat with her tongue. Within a few seconds she actually passes out – if she is upright at the start of the episode, she may topple over in a faint. If your child has this sort of tantrum, you will already know that they are terrifying to watch. For suggestions on coping with a breath-holding tantrum, see Practical Principles, right.

Dealing With a Biter

Some children bite hard when they are in a tantrum, and this is usually extremely painful for the recipient. This four-stage plan is a useful approach to stopping a child from biting:

1. **Understand.** Often the victim is someone who just happens to be in the wrong place at the wrong time. That's why you might find that your toddler tries to sink her teeth into you during a rage, even though you are not necessarily connected to the source of her frustration.
2. **Restrain.** Biting cannot be ignored: you have to restrain a biter because of the hurt she creates. As soon as she starts to bite – or when you think she is

If your child bites, you must make sure she clearly understands the pain she has caused.

about to bite – hold her gently but firmly by her arms and say 'No, don't bite.' Repeat this message several times if necessary. Never bite her back, as that simply encourages her to bite even more.

3. **Remove.** If she has started biting before you reach her, gently but firmly remove her physically from the person she is biting, while giving those verbal instructions at the same time. Lightly restrain her in this way each time she bites. She'll probably remain in a foul temper but your loud, clear instructions make her think about her biting behaviour.
4. **Explain.** Once the biting episode is over – even if you have prevented the actual biting – sit with your tearful toddler and explain to her that her biting hurts. Tell her 'When you bite your friend it makes her cry' or 'I feel very sore and unhappy when you bite me.' She needs to grasp the practical implications of her behaviour.

Questions and Answers

When my toddler bites, she is not in a temper. In fact, she usually has a smile on her face. Why does she do this?

In this instance, your child bites because she thinks it is amusing – she genuinely doesn't grasp that this causes pain to the other person. Gently restrain her if necessary, and at the same time make sure she knows how much distress she creates for the recipient. Do this every single time she bites playfully.

My child is almost 4 years old and she still has breath-holding tantrums. When will this stop?

This type of tantrum stops at around the age of 5 years, and certainly by the time of starting school. By then, a child has more self-control and dislikes the feelings associated with a breath-holding episode. In addition, social pressure from peers makes breath holding inappropriate. You'll find, therefore, that your child stops completely within the next year or so.

5 Practical Principles

1. **Stay calm.**
   Your child won't hurt herself during a breath-holding episode – the second she starts to pass out, she spontaneously starts to draw breath again.

2. **Keep her safe.**
   The biggest danger is that your child will bang her head or body when she faints, so make sure you are there to grab her when she starts to tumble.

3. **Prevent if possible.**
   As with any form of tantrum, prevention is the best approach. Try to nip the tantrum in the bud before it escalates to the breath-holding stage.

4. **Encourage breathing.**
   Some parents blow hard into the back of their child's throat or hook their index finger and use it to pull their child's tongue gently forward.

5. **Soothe her.**
   The chances are that your child will be very upset as soon as she regains full consciousness. Give her a big cuddle and soothe her until she settles.

Fears and Phobias

There is hardly a child who isn't afraid sometimes, depending on the circumstances. In fact, children can be afraid of almost anything at all. Fortunately, most childhood fears are mild, temporary and manageable – with some parental help and encouragement.

In contrast, a phobia is much less common – surveys estimate that less than five per cent of all children have a genuine phobia. A phobia is different from a fear in a number of ways, including:

- **Severity.** A child with a phobia worries even when the focus of her anxiety is not present. For instance, a child who is afraid of dogs will be troubled when she nears one in the street, whereas a child with a phobia about dogs would be upset just thinking about these animals.
- **Resistance.** In most instances, childhood fears are temporary and often ease with some structured support and guidance. Phobias, however, are much more resistant to change, and they tend to last for years rather than months.
- **Impact.** Every fear has an effect on a child's life – for instance, she may try to avoid going to parties because she is afraid of meeting new people. A phobia, on the other hand, is more pervasive – for instance, she doesn't want to leave the house at all in case she meets an unfamiliar adult.

Common Fears

Of course, every child is different, but here are some of the most common fears that occur in childhood:

- **Small animals.** Many children dislike small animals that move unpredictably – that's why animals such as insects and hamsters often create such terror in young minds.

Fear of mess and dirt, as with most other fears, usually lessens and disappears as your child matures.

Love, patience and reassurance are the best way to respond to your child's fears.

- **Darkness.** Total darkness fills some children with terror – they become afraid the moment the light goes out at night.
- **Cats and dogs.** Memories of a snarling dog or scratching cat can make a child afraid whenever she sees one of these household pets.
- **Dirt.** Some children are very neat and fastidious. The sight of dirt on their hands or clothes makes them afraid and upset.
- **Water.** Nobody likes to get soapy water in their eyes during hair washing, but a child can be so afraid of this that she screams hysterically in the bath.
- **Injury.** While many children are daredevils without any fear at all, many others are frightened to explore at all in case they hurt themselves.
- **Failure.** A child can be so afraid of failing at something that she prefers not to try anything new at all – this protects her from the source of her concern.
- **Loss of love.** You know that you don't care for your child any less when you are angry with her, but she might fear that she'll lose your love at these moments.
- **Separation.** A child under the age of 3 or 4 years often shows real fear when she realizes her parent is about to leave her with another carer.

Changing Fears With Age

1 year: Fear of strangers is common during the toddler stage. That's why your child buries her face against your thigh when an unfamiliar adult whom you know tries to talk to her.

2 years: The emphasis on toilet training at this age can create a fear of the toilet bowl (which looks huge to her). The fear of separation can also emerge at this age as she first attends a parent-and-toddler group.

3 years: Growth in her imagination at this age often results in fear of 'things in the dark'. Terror of cats and dogs is also common because she is spending more time outdoors.

4 years: She can't help but compare herself to her friends, especially if she goes to nursery. This can make her afraid of being less competent than her friends and the thought of not matching up to them frightens her.

5 years: Fears tend to be related to real-life challenges such as a medical examination or visit to the dentist. This fear is based on a previous experience that has upset her.

6 years: Now that school plays such an important role in her life, fears about class tests can emerge. All it takes is one poor grade to make your child afraid of the next one.

7 years: Friendships matter more than ever and fear of social rejection is often very strong. Your child may be very worried, for example, in case she is not invited to a classmate's birthday party.

8 years: It is unlikely that a new fear will appear at this point in a child's life. She has gained control over most of her previous fears and is more confident about dealing with fear when it arises.

strategy: Spotting Signs of Fear

The first stage in helping your frightened child is to recognize that she is afraid! This may not be as easy as you might think, because the actual signs of fear depend on your individual child. You may know when she is frightened because, say, she starts to sob quietly or clings tightly to you, and you have probably developed your own ways to get her through these difficult episodes. However, it is not always easy to tell when a child is frightened.

Children can express fear in many different ways and it can be difficult to read your child's behaviour. Of course, your child may simply tell you 'I don't like this, I'm afraid of it', but you may find that she demonstrates her fear through her behaviour rather than through her words. The signs of fear are not always obvious and they may include any of the following behaviours:

- A normally fluent child starts to stutter.
- Her appetite drops dramatically.
- She becomes lethargic and reluctant to play with her friends.
- She becomes disruptive.
- She starts to perspire profusely.

Your child might not immediately tell you that she is afraid, so look for the tell-tale indications that she may be frightened.

In relaxed, controlled circumstances you can help your child confront her fear, which is a big step towards overcoming it.

In some instances, a child is too anxious to admit to her parents that she is afraid of something as she thinks they may laugh at her. No child wants to be ridiculed, and therefore concealment of the fear can become a child's strategy for dealing with it. If the fear remains, however, it will eventually show through. When it does, respond immediately.

Questions and Answers

Can a child use imagery to overcome a fear?

There is some evidence that this can work even with children as young as 3 years. The technique involves the child imagining that she has confronted the source of her fear – for instance, that she has patted the dog or sat the school test successfully. This mental rehearsal, which takes places entirely in her imagination, helps prepare her psychologically for the experience when she next encounters it in the real world.

My 6-year-old has been afraid of insects for years. Nothing seems to help. Should I just accept this?

Keep trying to help her. If you stop encouraging her, then her fear will probably become habitual, which makes it even harder to change. Some fears are more resistant to change than others, so be prepared to persist with your support. She'll continue to work at beating her fear as long as she knows you are working with her, too.

5 Practical Principles

1 Take your child seriously.
You may find it amusing to think that she is terrified of an insect but the fear is very real to your child. Avoid ridicule – she cannot be joked out of it. Instead, let her see that you are sympathetic and there to help her. She needs to know that you are firmly on her side with your support.

2 Give lots of reassurance.
Tell your child repeatedly that she has nothing to fear, that she is totally safe and that everything will be fine. Do this as often as you need to, until her confidence starts to improve. Your reassurance boosts her emotional strength, eventually giving her the resolve to beat her fear.

3 Aim for confrontation.
She won't learn to overcome her fear unless she tries to confront it. Make sure that she doesn't avoid the focus of her fear – for instance, she may ask to stay at home because your neighbour keeps a dog. Although avoidance might be an easy solution at first, it doesn't help her to deal effectively with her fear.

4 Teach her to relax.
When you see your child tense up with fear, encourage her to unclench her hand and arm muscles, relax her facial expression and breathe more easily. Practise this regularly each day with your child at home. These physical changes help her to cope with her fear because they induce calmness.

5 Tackle her fear with her.
Show your child that she can beat her fear by going through the dreaded event beside her. Your presence and encouragement gives her the confidence to, say, climb up to the next level of the climbing frame. It's amazing how she draws psychological strength just from your presence.

strategy: Managing Fears

If you know that your child is due to face something that usually frightens her – for example, a visit to the doctor, a class test, a journey on a plane – don't just leave things to chance. There is no point in simply trusting to luck. Instead, help your child prepare in advance so that she feels confident and ready emotionally to beat her fear.

Consider the following strategies:

- **Early warning.** Suppose, for instance, that your child has a visit to the dentist next week and you know that she was very afraid the last time – so give her a few day's notice. This allows both you and her time to develop a plan for managing her fear.
- **Stay calm.** Knowing that she is likely to be afraid probably makes you tense, too. However, your tensions feed her fear. You will be more help to your frightened child by remaining totally calm yourself.
- **Practise useful techniques.** Encourage your child to prepare by practising fear-reducing strategies such as muscle and breathing relaxation or positive self-talk (in which she tells herself that she is not afraid). Go over these with her at home.
- **Praise progress.** Almost certainly she will be less frightened than expected because of the preparation. Give her lots of praise for being calmer during the potentially frightening experience. Ask her to recall the strategies that helped her.

Fear of the Dark

Fear of the dark is very common during childhood. Your child has such a lively imagination that she easily conjures up images of ghosts and things that go bump in the night. She may complain furiously when you try to turn off her bedroom light at night.

As well as the planned use of a night light in her room (see page 67), reassure her that she has nothing to fear from darkness. It could be helpful for you to sit with her once she is in bed and the light is off, and chat for a few minutes until she settles.

Night fears take many forms so find out whether your child is afraid of monsters, the dark itself or finding her way to the toilet. Then adopt an appropriate strategy.

Questions and Answers

My child grabs tightly on to my hand every time we enter a room in which there are other children. Should I insist that she acts more independently in these situations?

She obviously feels afraid, at least in the early moments of meeting other children, so there is no harm at this stage in letting her use you as an emotional support. Once she has been in the room for a minute or two, gently but firmly encourage her to let go of your hand.

How can I reduce my child's fear of medical examinations? She howls every time I have to take her to the doctor.

Reassure her that she has nothing to worry about. Explain that the doctor won't do anything without first discussing it with you and with her. Let her have a look around the surgery for a few minutes while you chat to the doctor, and then ask her to sit beside you. If you know that the doctor has reward stickers for young patients, let her know that she'll get one.

Sometimes a child is anxious about darkness because she is unsure about finding her way to the toilet from her bedroom if she wakes in the middle of the night. Leaving a light on in the hall outside the child's bedroom often solves this problem. Walk the route with her just before she goes to bed, as this will act as a further boost to her confidence.

Bathtime Blues

The slippery surface of the bath, the varied temperature of the water and the worry of soap suds running into her eyes are typical fears associated with your child's evening bath. She may also be frightened because the bath seems so big. See Practical Principles on the right for tips on coping with this fear.

5 Practical Principles

Here are some suggestions for alleviating a child's fear of bathtime.

❶ **Make the bath as comfortable as possible for your child.**
For instance, buy a non-slip bathmat and check the temperature of the water very carefully before she climbs in.

❷ **Explain these measures to her before bathtime.**
She will be reassured to be told that these safety steps are in place.

❸ **Use a hair-washing hood.**
This large plastic ring fits over your child's head, preventing soap suds from slipping into her eyes. Wash the soap away towards the back of her head.

❹ **Give her lots of bath toys.**
Playing with these makes the whole experience enjoyable rather than frightening for your child.

❺ **Don't rush it.**
Uncomfortable water splashes, slips and other frightening experiences are less likely when you bathe your child at a relaxed pace. Try not to be in a hurry.

Optimist or Pessimist?

Optimism is a marvellous quality in children, just as it is in adults. Life is so much more enjoyable for your child when she is upbeat, and sees the positives. Remember when a picnic was cancelled because of bad weather? You expected tears or temper, but she was happy as she could now play with her new jigsaw.

Pessimistic children, on the other hand, see only the downside of everything. No matter what good comes their way, they somehow manage to find a flaw in it. When the inevitable problems do occur, they simply accept this as their lot in life. In addition, a pessimistic child:

- Cries much more easily when confronting a problem or minor difficulty.
- Gives up more easily when faced with a new challenge.
- Is more easily upset by changes in her routine either at home or at the nursery.
- Takes longer to come out of an unhappy mood.
- Is more easily upset by unkind remarks from others.
- Is less likely to persist with a demanding game or puzzle toy.

Building Optimism

- **Concentrate on making her feel good about herself.** This keeps her optimism high and makes her ready emotionally for problems and challenges that might come her way. Make a point of talking to your child about her skills, talents, abilities and characteristics, all the features that make her the wonderful person she is. Let her

If you help your child find solutions to problems from a young age then she will adopt this attitude herself.

5 Reasons why optimism vanishes

❶ **Poor self-esteem.**
When a child doesn't value herself, she expects the world to go against her. She struggles to see the bright side of any situation.

❷ **Limited confidence.**
A child who feels buoyant about herself and her abilities is able to cope with the daily challenges that come her way. Lack of confidence weakens this ability.

Children get disproportionally upset over small things so whilst you must not make light of a problem, help keep a sense of perspective.

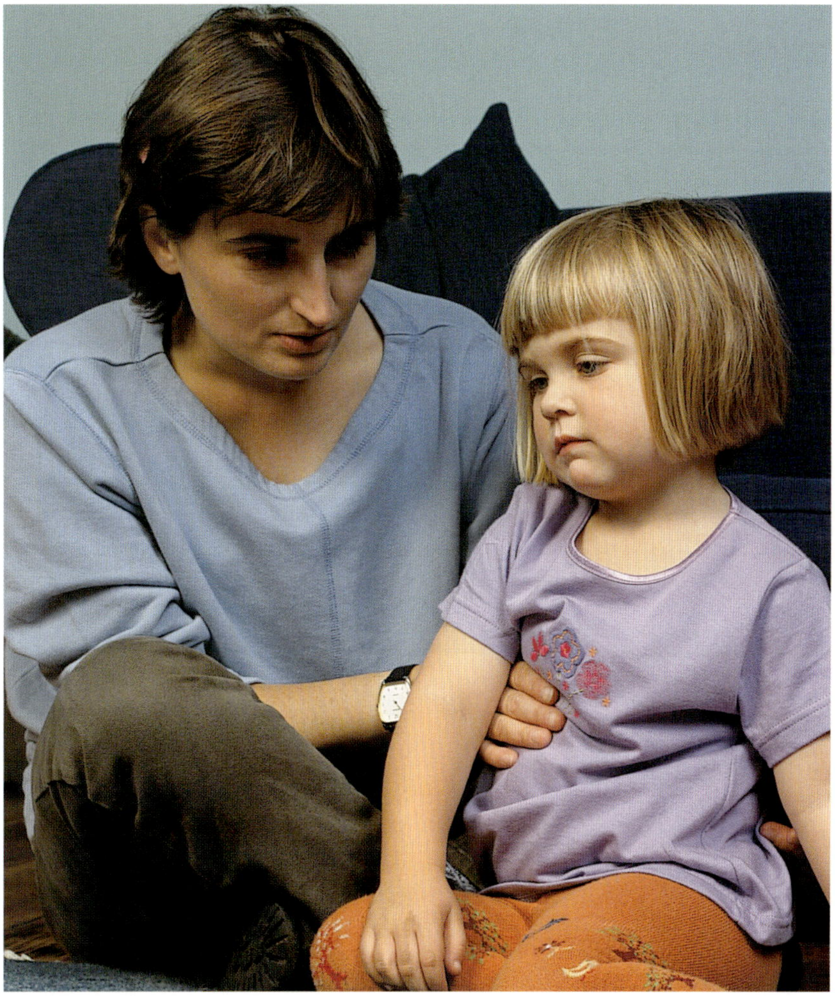

see that you are interested in her. Give her attention when she tries to show off her latest achievement. Your enthusiasm makes her feel that she matters, and a child who has that sort of confidence usually has a stronger sense of optimism.

- **Teach your child to find solutions to problems.** Pessimism replaces optimism when she thinks that there is no way out of her predicament, whatever that is at the time. That's why she needs you to develop her solution-based approach to life. For instance, when she sobs to you that she has misplaced her favourite toy, suggest that she searches for it systematically rather than in a haphazard way – the toy will turn up eventually. Focusing on solutions instead of problems gives your child more control over her life, which in turn boosts her optimism.
- **Encourage her sense of humour.** Perhaps it is not particularly funny when her ice cream accidentally slips from her hand on to the ground – but there is an amusing side to the incident. After all, that sort of experience is the cornerstone of slapstick comedy. Laughter can replace tears in many situations – all it takes is a shift in perspective to see the funny side of life.

Positive Reinforcement

Give your child lots of praise when she demonstrates optimism – for instance, when she reassures you that her toy can be repaired even though it is broken at the moment. Your approval reinforces her positive outlook on life. Similarly, do your best to set a good example yourself. Young children often take their lead from their parents. Your attitude to life and the way you respond when facing minor hurdles provides a model for your child to copy. Optimism is catching!

❸ Fights between mum and dad.
You can hardly expect your child to have a positive view of the world in general if the atmosphere at home is tense and strained.

❹ Unhappiness.
A happy child is almost always an optimist; conversely, a sad child is almost always a pessimist. It's hard to look forward brightly when you are feeling miserable.

❺ Troubled friendships.
Your child begins to have self-doubts when friendships become awkward. Peer rejection is linked to pessimism.

strategy: Reacting to a 'Show-off'

Although some children shun any public attention, the majority like to display their talents in front of others, whether in an end-of-term show or to a small audience at home. This is a great way to boost your child's confidence. However, a few children will grab the limelight at any opportunity. The 'show-off' child wants attention all the time, and does anything she can to make sure others notice her. She often isn't as talented as she believes and doesn't always have the ability to merit the attention she craves.

Giving your child plenty of attention at home will make her less likely to seek it at school or with friends.

A child who shows off in front of others does so for a variety of reasons, including:

- **Self-pride.** Quite simply, she is delighted with her achievements and wants the whole world to know about them.
- **Self-doubt.** Ironically, a child might show off in front of her peers precisely because she lacks confidence. This is her desperate attempt to gain their approval.
- **Attention.** A child who wants more attention than she currently receives will show off in order to gain extra notice from others around her.
- **Antagonism.** Sometimes she shows off deliberately in order to antagonize others – it's her way of getting back at those who annoy her.
- **Aspirations.** Showing off helps her fulfil her dreams. She doesn't even have to be especially talented – she just wants to be a performer.

The problem with showing off is that most onlookers react negatively. Repeated public demonstrations of ability (whether real or imagined) simply tend to irritate peers and can create social difficulties as they won't want to be with her. The show-off wants admiration, yet often ends up with rejection.

Too Confident

An over-confident child generally crash-lands with a bump, usually because she overestimates her talents and then fails to meet the particular challenge she tackled. You have to strike a balance between developing your child's confidence and encouraging it so much that she develops an over-inflated sense of her own abilities.

One way to avoid the disappointments that are associated with over-confidence is to suggest that your child evaluates each challenge carefully before embarking on it. Another strategy is to analyse your child's successes and failures with her, to enable her to learn from what happened in each instance.

Questions and Answers

I can see my child's friends secretly smirking at her when she shows off the latest move she learned at her ballet class. How can I stop her without upsetting her?

It's best to be honest. Explain sensitively that her pals could become bored with her 'shows', even though you are very proud of her achievements. Suggest she keeps these demonstrations for you, unless her friends specifically ask for them (which is unlikely).

My child always pitches her expectations for school tests too high – then she ends up in tears with the lower result. What should I do?

Try to discover the reason for her poor performance. Perhaps she does need to develop a more realistic perspective, but it may be that she just struggles with timed exams. For example, she might have a problem giving answers under pressure or maybe she doesn't read the questions properly and then panics.

5 Practical Principles

1 Provide home opportunities.
Your child's need to show off is reduced by having opportunities to demonstrate her abilities at home. Arrange for her to give a small show to you or her siblings, instead of being so overt with her peers.

2 Give her insight.
Tactfully and sensitively explain to your child that while other people admire her talents, they eventually grow bored with those constant reminders. Encourage her to give others a chance to display their skills, too.

3 Suggest alternatives.
Teach her that she can gain approval in subtle ways, which are preferable to showing off. For instance, she can leave out photos of her drama show when visitors call round instead of insisting that she gives them a special live performance.

4 Give her attention.
Where a child shows off because she feels unnoticed, it can be helpful to give her more attention on a day-to-day basis. Taking interest in her all the time as a matter of routine reduces her desire for those occasional excessive displays.

5 Teach her to be responsive to others.
As well acknowledging her achievements, encourage her to consider the skills that other people have, too. Point out, for instance, that her sister is a wonderful piano player, just as she plays the flute beautifully.

strategy: Dealing with a Bossy Chil

Some children just love to boss everyone about, telling their friends exactly how to play the game or giving precise instructions for their parents and siblings to follow. But a bossy child soon finds that others don't want to play with him, so do what you can to help yours become less dominant with his peers.

A child who bosses other people usually does so because he:

- Loves the sensation that derives from being in charge of everyone else.
- Feels powerful and in control when he bosses people around.
- Likes things to be done exactly his way.
- Is very confident that he always has the very best solution.
- Fears that the other children will make the wrong choice in a given situation.
- Has a strong need for excessive structure and stability in his life.
- Lacks the confidence to cope when someone else gives instructions.

Your child's bossy behaviour can lead to the following problems because he:

- Does not recognize all the good qualities that are present in other people.
- Fails to listen to any ideas except those that he generates himself.
- Is likely to be socially isolated by his peers, who will eventually exclude him.
- Irritates other people with his lack of self-doubt.
- Is no fun to be with when he bosses other people around.
- Rarely learns from mistakes because he is so convinced he is right.
- Constantly voices his opinion even when it is not asked for.

Questions and Answers

Should I let my 5-year-old give in to my 2-year-old when he tries to boss him around?

Your older child obviously cares about his younger brother and perhaps even finds his assertiveness cute. He doesn't want to upset him, so he lets him push him around. In the long term, though, he should discourage his bossiness. Talk to him about some of the negative effects of your 2-year-old's bossy behaviour, especially in terms of his friendships with other children.

My 4-year-old goes on at me so much that I feel like screaming. How can I get him to stop?

As well as the range of strategies suggested (see Practical Principles, right), you probably need an occasional break from him when he is this demanding. Ask your partner – or a friend or relative – to look after him while you rest for a couple of hours. A short spell away from your child recharges your emotional batteries.

Dealing with Bossiness

Try the following strategies for dealing with a bossy child:

- Encourage him to understand the effect of his behaviour on others.
- Suggest that he listens to what others have to say, before he acts.
- Tell him to give others a chance to air their views instead of shouting them down.
- Advise him to give his friend a turn to be in charge for a change.

A child who is confident without being dominating will be able to build good relationships with adults as well as his peers.

- Ask him to imagine what it would be like to have a very bossy friend.
- Play a game with him in which he has to follow your directions throughout.
- Explain the practical implications of his bossiness on his friends and family.

Nagging

Some children just don't give up. They are determined to get what they want so they persist in nagging until you surrender. You start off with good intentions but the constant, repetitive demands prove too much and you let your child do what he wants because you have no more resistance. However, do not despair: there are some strategies you can use to tackle the situation more effectively (see Practical Principles, right).

5 Practical Principles

1 Ignore him when possible.
Do not let your child's repeated demands get to you. Just ignore him. Of course, that can be very difficult, but try to ignore him anyway.

2 Think ahead.
Tell yourself that the more you let him wear you down, the more he'll do this in the future. Acknowledge that acceding to his demands gives you a respite for only a few minutes, until his next endlessly repeated request. Think of the long term.

3 Compromise occasionally.
There is nothing wrong with reaching a compromise with your child sometimes – say, when he has been nagging you all day to let him stay up later that night. Explain why you are making the compromise this time.

4 Anticipate his wishes.
If you expect him to nag at you to, say, take him swimming the following evening, tell him the night before that you plan to take him there the next day. This demonstrates that he doesn't need to wear you down to get what he wants.

5 Give him choices.
See if he behaves more reasonably when you offer him a choice of, say, three toys that he can have for his birthday. Instead of trying to wear you down to get what he wants, he has to take responsibility himself.

Fear of Failure

Nobody likes failure – neither you nor your child. He is very fragile emotionally when success eludes him. One minute he is having great fun playing with toys, the next he is sitting in tears because the jigsaw is too demanding for him. His head hangs and he feels thoroughly dejected. That's a normal reaction.

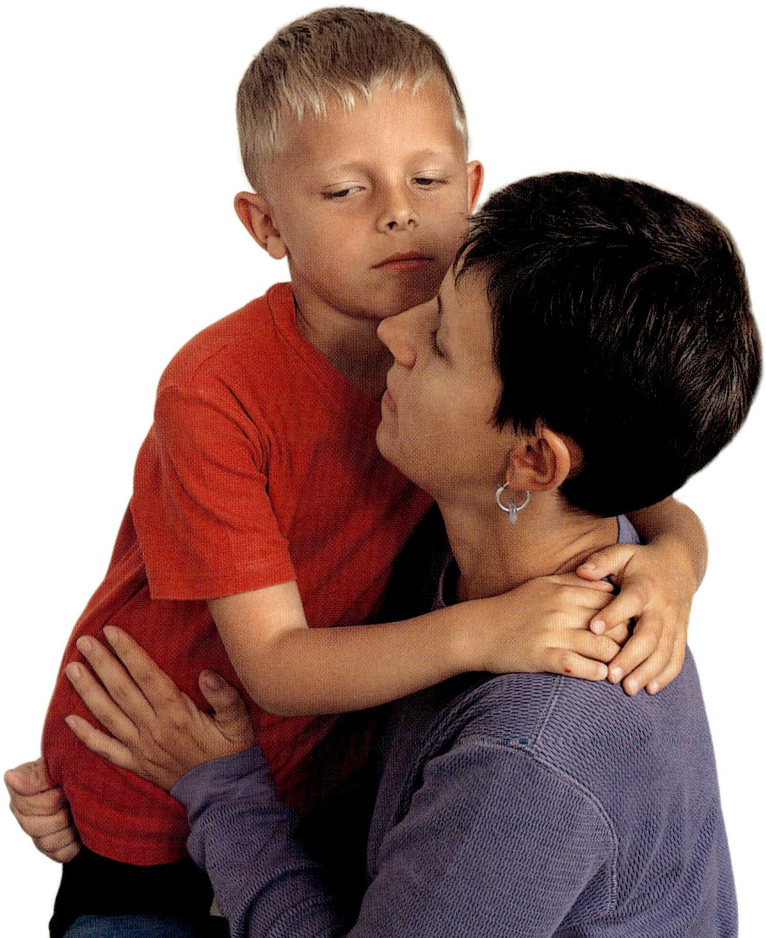

However, if your child actually starts to fear failure rather than just reacting badly to it, then other psychological problems also emerge:

- **He won't want to tackle anything new**. Your child would rather miss out on an activity than run the risk of failing at it. He misses out on opportunities for enjoyment, learning and personal development.
- **He becomes very self-critical.** His expectation of failure leads him to believe he is full of inadequacies; he even starts to criticize his successes, because he believes they have no value.
- **He grows very anxious about challenges he can't avoid.** Typical examples here are school examinations.
- **He loses the ability to get fun out of play.** The lack of self-confidence associated with fear of failure, coupled with the underlying anxiety, means that your child stops enjoying himself because he worries so much about not coping.

Your Attitude

Success matters in life, but failure is not the end of the world. In many instances, failure can be used

While you may share your child's disappointment, he needs you to be positive and help him recover his self-esteem.

5 Ways to turn failure into success

❶ Emphasize your child's effort as well as his success.

Your child cannot ensure success in competitive events (because he can't make himself better than he is), but he can ensure that he tries his best. That's why you should value his effort more than his achievements.

❷ Highlight his strengths.

He needs you to spell out his strong points and positive characteristics to him, otherwise he simply focuses on the negative dimensions. This fear of failure is reduced when his self-esteem is at a high level.

Practical strategies, like extra help with schoolwork, are often the best way to help your child tackle failure.

positively, as an opportunity to develop new skills. Your child's attitude to success and failure depends on yours. Try asking yourself the following questions:

- Do I show an excessive level of disappointment when my child doesn't achieve his target?
- Do I tend to focus on his failures rather than his successes?
- Do I place more importance on my child's results than I do on the effort he has made?
- Do I encourage him to conceal his failures from my friends?
- Do I compare him to other children who are more successful than he is?
- Do I punish my child when I think he could have done better?

If you answer 'yes' to most of these, you could be contributing to, or even creating, his fear of failure. By all means have a positive and encouraging attitude towards attainments, but do not value success above all else. A child who has that perspective on life always reacts badly to failure.

Regression Under Pressure

Children experience psychological pressure and stress in the same way as adults. Although fear of failure is one stress in childhood, there are plenty of others, too, such as worry about parental fights, anxiety about friendships, concern about social isolation and even the pressure of tackling the school curriculum.

Your child learns to cope with pressure through experience. In the meantime, however, you may find that he 'regresses' when stressed: that is, he returns to an earlier stage of development. In this completely instinctive strategy of psychological self-defence, he begins to behave like a younger child does. For instance, he might:

- Start to wet himself, even though he was previously dry.
- Begin to suck his thumb as he did when he was a toddler.
- Use an immature form of speech even though he can talk fluently.
- Cling tightly as if he is afraid to leave you.

Try to recognize regressive behaviour when it appears. Remember, it is a sign that your child is under stress – he is not deliberately trying to be disruptive. Once you discover the source of stress and ease the pressure, you'll find that his regressive behaviour vanishes as quickly as it arrived.

❸ Analyse the cause of failures.
The chances are that he could have obtained a better result if he had approached the activity in a different way. Go over the strategies he used, in order to identify alternative approaches for the next time.

❹ Give lots of encouragement.
Fight your child's instinct to give up. Persuade him to try again, no matter how much success has eluded him so far. Your encouragement boosts his willingness and determination.

❺ Offer sympathy and solutions.
Be sympathetic to him about his disappointment, soothe him, and mop up his tears – then tell him you are sure he will score higher next time if you help him prepare.

strategy: Comforting a Cry Baby

It's fine for your child to cry. Both boys and girls are entitled to shed tears occasionally when things go wrong for them, like the time your child burst out crying when he banged his knee against the coffee table or when he discovered that he was not invited to his friend's birthday party. Crying is a normal stress reaction, but sometimes a child will shed tears too easily – a 'cry baby' turns on the tears as effortlessly as smiling.

Questions and Answers

How can I make my child more resilient to the knocks he experiences in everyday life? His confidence is so easily dented.

The problem arises because he places too much importance on these incidents, so encourage him to keep minor upsets in perspective. Remind him that the actual effects of these events are small and suggest that he should try not to become so upset by them. Repeat this to your child each time you see his confidence drop.

My 6-year-old turns on the tears like a tap when he is with his grandmother, who gives in to him. How can I stop him taking advantage in this way?

There are two strategies to use in this situation. First, explain to his grandmother that he is using tears deliberately to get what he wants, and emphasise that he doesn't do this at home. Second, have a chat with your son about behaving like a 'big boy' when he is with his grandmother, instead of pretending to cry in order to get his own way.

In most instances, a child cries easily like this because he has learned that it is an effective strategy for gaining sympathy and attention – experience has taught him that all he needs to do is shed a few tears and his parents will rally around him as though he were in the middle of a truly dreadful trauma. To stop your 'cry baby' sobbing so often, consider the following suggestions:

- **Don't react to his tears so quickly.** Work on the assumption that he is not really upset and that he cries just to grab your attention. Giving a measured response to his tears discourages this habit.
- **Reinforce mature behaviour.** When your child copes with a minor disappointment without resorting to tears, give him lots of praise. Point out how delighted you are at his mature reaction on this particular occasion.
- **Ask him to try harder.** Be direct with your child – ask him to cry less. Tell him you think he could make more of an effort to cope without tears. Explain that other children will eventually make fun of him if he continues to behave in this way.
- **Explain the consequences.** It may be helpful to point out to your 'cry baby' that people don't take his tears seriously because he cries so often. Add that they won't know when he is genuinely distressed and so they won't help him when he really needs it.

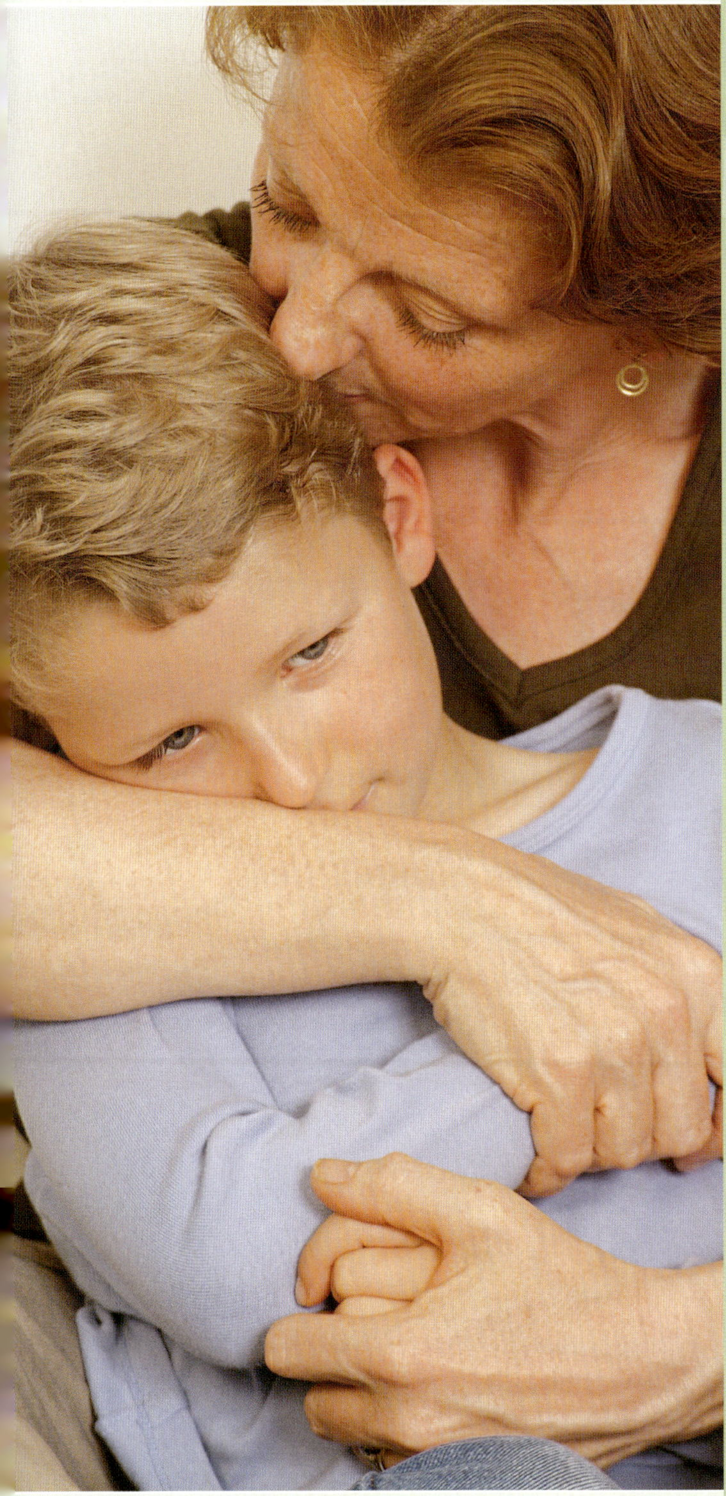

If crying has become a habit, continue to be loving and supportive but explain why self-control is needed.

5 Practical Principles

❶ **Be supportive and interested.**
Your child feels good about himself when you take an interest in everything he does. Talk to him about his experiences each day, discuss his likes and dislikes, and be ready to offer advice and guidance when necessary. Your interest makes him feel important and special.

❷ **Encourage his development.**
Try to arrange for lots of stimulation and play activities that allow him to develop his talents to the full. Success in these activities boosts his self-esteem, especially when he realizes that you are pleased with him. Every child is good at something, so help him find those hidden skills.

❸ **Let him know you love him.**
He never tires of hearing you tell him that you think he is marvellous. Your child values your opinion greatly. This applies as much to a school-aged child as it does to a toddler. Voice your positive feelings, even if he appears totally uninterested in your loving remarks.

❹ **Avoid comparisons.**
Telling him that his brother – or his best friend – manages tasks more effectively than he does won't have a positive effect on his self-confidence. The opposite outcome is more likely. Comparisons usually make a child feel worse about himself, not better. That's why it is best to avoid them altogether.

❺ **Use criticism positively.**
Virtually all negative comments can be expressed in a way that leaves your child's self-esteem intact. For example, instead of saying 'I'm fed up with you for being so noisy' you could say 'You are usually so well-behaved that I'm very surprised you made such a disturbance with your friends today.'

strategy: Giving up a Comforter

Your child clings to that tattered old cot blanket or grubby old soft toy that she has had since she was a baby because it makes her feel good. She loves the familiar smell and feel of the object. In fact, it doesn't have to be an object that is the comforter: it can be a habit, such as thumb sucking, hair twiddling or even using a baby's bottle to drink her milk long after she is able to use an open cup. In every instance, the action gives psychological comfort to your child which is why she will want to take it with her wherever she goes.

Pros and Cons

There are good and bad sides to a child's use of a comforter, so it may help you to think about these if you want to encourage your child to give up using hers. Your child's use of a comforter can be a positive thing for the following reasons:

- Soothes her and helps her to relax when she is tense or distressed.
- Makes some everyday activities, such as watching television, more enjoyable.
- Enables her to get to sleep more easily at night when she cuddles up to it.
- Puts her at ease in unfamiliar situations, such as in a hotel room or staying with friends.
- Gives her courage to face challenges, such as a visit to the dentist.

However, on the negative side, your child's use of a comforter:

- Discourages her ability to face new challenges using her own resources.
- Creates organizational difficulties – for instance, when she insists it travels with her.
- Causes physical difficulties – for instance, thumb sucking could misshape her teeth.
- Can be unhealthy – for example, if she sucks a comforter that is dirty.
- Makes her look babyish and immature.

Questions and Answers

Has my child's use of a comforter anything to do with feelings of insecurity?

This is unlikely. In fact, the opposite may be true – psychological research has confirmed that a child who has a comforter before she reaches school age tends to get on better with her classmates once she is at school, and is more likely to be outgoing and confident. It could be, therefore, that using a comforter is actually good for your child.

How can I persuade my 3-year-old to let me wash her favourite cuddly teddy? It's absolutely filthy but she won't let it out of her sight.

One solution is to get her involved in the cleaning process. For instance, she can help add soap powder to the warm water and can push her teddy until it is submerged. She can then help with the rinsing and even watch it turning round in the tumbledryer. Being involved in this way reduces her anxiety about letting the teddy be cleaned.

It really is up to you whether or not to allow your child's continued use of a comforter or comfort habit. You have to decide what is right for your child, your family and you. Most children gradually give up their use of a comforter anyway, until by the time they start school they have discarded it completely. However, if you do decide to discourage her habit there are several strategies you can try (see Practical Principles, right).

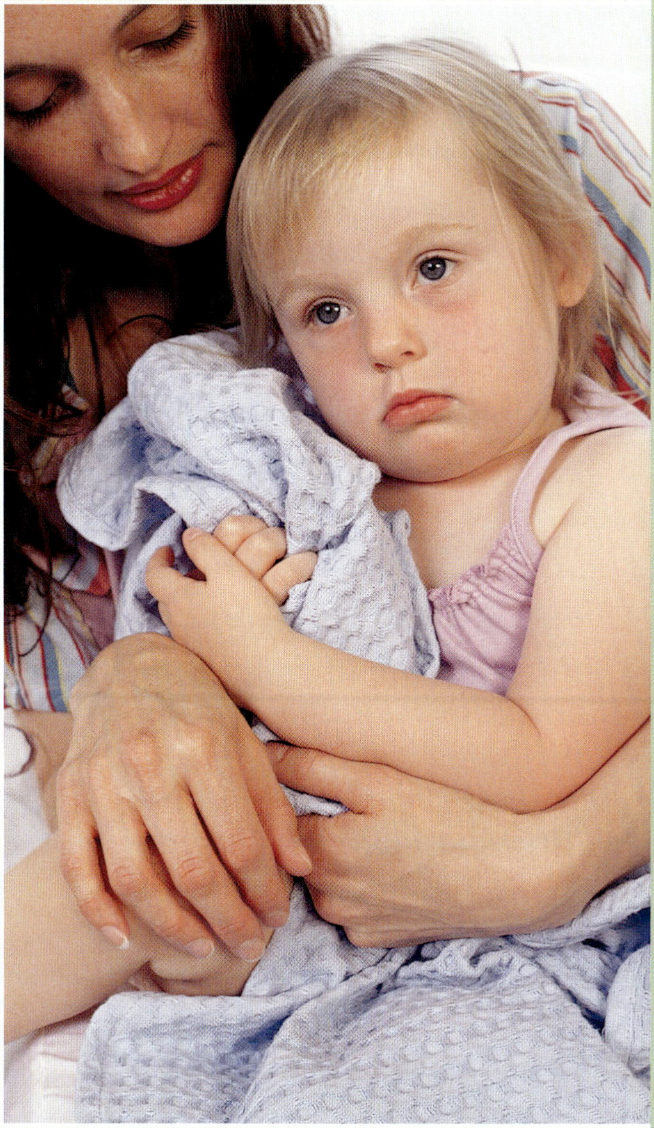

Comforters like a favourite blanket can be very useful for putting young children at ease in strange situations.

5 Practical Principles

❶ **Work with your child, not in opposition.**
You need her cooperation when trying to wean her off a comforter. Do your best to avoid unnecessary confrontations – her determination to persist in using the object simply becomes more entrenched if you start fighting with her over it.

❷ **Don't make fun of her.**
Making comments such as 'You look like a baby the way you suck that blanket at night' or 'Your younger sister doesn't suck her thumb any more' just makes her want to use her comforter even more. These taunts from you make her feel anxious.

❸ **Set a small target to begin with.**
It is unreasonable for you to expect your child to give up her comforter the moment you decide she is too old for it. She cannot break a habit overnight. A more effective strategy is to suggest that she tries to avoid using the comforter for a specific amount of time – perhaps an hour at first.

❹ **Build on her successes.**
Once she manages to do without her comfort object or habit for that amount of time, gradually extend the period by a few minutes each day. Her enthusiasm for giving up the comforter completely is enhanced by those early successes. Progress is slow and steady.

❺ **Reinforce her achievement.**
Tell her how happy you are with her new behaviour. Find ways to reward her for not using the comforter, such as verbal praise or announcing her progress to her grandparents. Make a fuss of this change even if she only reduces her use of the comforter by what you judge to be a small amount.

Born to Learn

Your child starts to learn from the moment she enters the world – she reaches, touches, tastes, smells, watches and constantly tries to discover new things. Her curiosity begins at birth and continues throughout life. She is thirsty for stimulation and loves acquiring new concepts. Your child truly is born to learn.

Through play, your growing child learns about her surroundings; she utilizes her movement and physical skills; she practises her creativity; she increases her problem-solving skills by tackling new games and puzzles; she progresses her language skills by interacting with others her own age.

Encouraging Learning and Problem-solving

Bear in mind that your child learns spontaneously, partly driven by her natural curiosity and partly through everyday experience at home and with her friends. However, there is lots you can do to stimulate these problem-solving skills as well:

- **Encourage your child to have a broad range of varied play activities.** She learns new and different concepts depending on the type of play. Each play activity will contribute in its own way to her learning.
- **Show her solutions when she is stuck.** Self-discovery is a vital part of learning. However, there is no point in letting your child struggle fruitlessly: be prepared to show her the solution occasionally.
- **Support her learning without pushing too hard.** If you want her to succeed with a learning activity that is too challenging, encourage her to take a short break instead of insisting that she perseveres.
- **Choose toys for her that are appropriate for her particular level of development and understanding.** When your child perceives the play activity as too demanding, she will give up

Children love to discover things for themselves so find some activities he can do without your help.

without really trying. Match games and toys to her abilities.

- **Allow your child to have lots of repetition with learning tasks.** Repetition enables her to consolidate ideas learned before. This boosts her motivation for learning the next concept.
- **Take an interest in her school work.** You can help her with literacy and numeracy activities. This underlies the importance of this form of learning.
- **Talk to your child about the day's activities and events.** This stimulates her speech and language development, which underpins much of her learning and teaches her to frame her ideas coherently.
- **Use television purposefully so that she watches quality programmes.** The careful selection of child-centred programmes can add to your child's knowledge.
- **Answer her questions appropriately.** Her constant questions help her to acquire new information. Although they can be tiring for you, answer them as best you can.

There are simple ways for children to explore the natural world, such as doing bark rubbings.

Age by Stage

Your child's problem-solving skills and learning abilities develop along the following lines:

1 week
- Grasps items placed in her hand, in a reflex reaction.
- Focuses on an object 20–25 cm (8–10 in) from her face.
- Tries to look at you when you speak to her.
- Recognizes the smell of her own mother's milk.

1 year
- Understands basic directions, involving only one action.
- Copies you when you bang two wooden blocks together.
- Points at an object with her finger.
- Says her first word around her first birthday.

2 years
- Opens a screw-together toy to obtain a smaller toy inside.
- Uses at least two dozen spoken words, often in short sentences.
- Is probably toilet-trained during the daytime.
- Gets involved in imaginative, dressing-up play.

3 years
- Recognizes several different colours.
- Knows the difference between 'big' and 'small'.
- Can copy a circle using a pencil or a crayon.
- Manages to complete a small jigsaw without help.

4 years
- Has a definite sense of humour.
- Names at least two primary colours.
- Uses language to describe her basic ideas and feelings.
- Understands basic time sequences – for instance, that morning comes before night.

5 years
- Recognizes and names numbers up to ten.
- Is capable of drawing a detailed picture of a house.
- Can identify the name of one or two coins.
- Can write the first few letters of her name.

5–8 years

Subsequent progress in learning and problem-solving skills between the ages of 5 and 8 years is connected to the school curriculum, and her progress is measured regularly by the school.

Much of classroom problem-solving occurs in groups – she learns a lot by listening and talking to her peers.

strategy: Aiding Concentration

Your child's ability to concentrate – that is, to deliberately focus her attention – changes as she grows. First, it becomes more active rather than passive. Initially, your child's attention is drawn passively to an object that captures her interest, but by the time she is 2 or 3 years old she starts to concentrate in a more controlled, systematic way. Second, she is able to filter out background noise more effectively, and is therefore less susceptible to distractions.

If you sit with your child you may find that she concentrates for longer on what she is doing.

Bear in mind, however, that everybody's concentration has limits. No matter how hard your child tries to concentrate, some information is likely to slip past her – that's why repetition is useful when she learns new concepts. Although boys and girls tend to have a similar ability to concentrate during the pre-school years, more boys than girls have difficulties with concentration in school.

Lack of Staying Power

You might find yourself wishing that your child would persist with something for longer before giving up. Instead, she seems to have a defeatist attitude, ready to 'down tools' as soon as she can. This is more about lack of motivation than lack of concentration.

Resist the temptation to accuse your child of laziness when she gives up. A far more constructive approach would be for you to consider why she makes less effort than you want. If you can identify the reason behind her lack of staying power, you will be better placed to encourage it. Consider the following possible explanations for her lack of motivation to continue with an activity:

Reason: The activity is too advanced for her and she finds it difficult to complete.
Strategy: Find a task that is challenging, but within her capabilities.

Reason: She finds the activity boring and uninteresting.
Strategy: Ask her to identify something that grabs her interest and attention.

Questions and Answers

Is it best for my child to do her homework all at once or with breaks in between? She has difficulties with concentration.

Short pauses are very useful when a child struggles to maintain her focus. She probably works better when she concentrates for, say, 15 minutes, then takes a rest for 15 minutes, then works for another 15 minutes. The chances are that she makes more progress that way than if she works for the entire 45-minute period.

Are there any games I can play with my child to improve her concentration?

Basic memory games are helpful. For instance, put six pairs of playing cards face down, then ask your child to turn two cards at a time before turning them face down again – she has to find all the matching pairs. Another memory game is to place 20 objects on a tray, let your child look at them for one minute, then ask her to recall as many as she can.

Reason: She isn't making any progress with this activity.
Strategy: Redirect her towards a different activity that has the potential for progress.

Reason: She has a passive nature, and lacks drive and enthusiasm for most things.
Strategy: Continue to encourage her, but accept that she has this sort of personality.

Reason: She realizes she is not as good as her peers.
Strategy: Encourage her to try hard for her own sake, no matter the ability of her peers.

Reason: The homework doesn't fire her enthusiasm.
Strategy: See if her teacher can give different work.

5 Practical Principles

1 Cut out distractions.
Your child concentrates more easily on information in front of her when background noises – such as the television, loud music or her siblings shouting at each other – are eliminated. Try to reduce distractions where possible.

2 Organize her personal space.
She concentrates better when her work area is uncluttered and the objects around her are well organized. Encourage her to sit at a clear table when trying to concentrate on an activity.

3 Sit with your child.
Studies have shown that a child is more likely to concentrate for longer when one of her parents sits with her, even when that parent is actively engaged on a completely unrelated task.

4 Don't expect too much.
Remember that your child concentrates for shorter periods now than she will when she is older. You cannot reasonably expect her to sit at the same learning activity for hours without a break, especially if it is demanding.

5 Aim for gradual increases.
Your child's concentration increases in small stages. If she normally works at a task for, say, three minutes, encourage her to concentrate for an extra 30 seconds. Add on a few seconds in this way each time.

strategy: Encouraging Listening

Children under the age of 5 years are often not very good when it comes to listening to questions or instructions – your comments seem to pass over their heads. You know your child's understanding is good and yet she fails to respond when you ask her a question or ask her to do something for you. Getting annoyed with her seems to have no effect, so you need to exercise some patience with her.

Specific games can have a positive impact on your child's listening skills. For instance, ask your child to close her eyes and then identify the main sounds that she hears, or play a game in which she gains a point every time she hears, say, a bird call or a dog bark. Alternatively, you could make a tape of various sounds that occur in her world every day, then ask her to name as many of these as possible when you play the tape back to her.

Another game is to give her an instruction with several pieces of information in it, such as 'Go to your brother's bedroom, get the blue ball and the green sock, put the green sock in the kitchen and give me the blue ball.' As long as you keep this fun and light-hearted, she'll enjoy this listening game.

Selective Listening

There are times when you're not sure if your child really didn't hear what you said or if she 'chose' not to hear you – like the time you asked her to help wash the dishes and she showed no reaction whatsoever. This form of selective listening is more common in children aged 5 years and older – at this age she has an amazing ability to tune you out when she can't be bothered to listen to what you have to say!

In this situation, it is best to be direct with her – direct, but calm. You can feel very frustrated when you are convinced your child is deliberately 'turning a deaf ear' towards you. After all, she expects you to listen to her and yet she doesn't reciprocate. Try not to lose your temper with her. Instead, tell her that you think she is ignoring you, remind her that you treat her with respect and that therefore she should do the same, and ask her to listen more closely. Do this on every single occasion that she fails to hear your words. You'll get through to her in time.

Questions and Answers

Whenever I reprimand my child, she switches off and her facial expression glazes over. How can I get her to listen to me?

Perhaps she is so used to your reprimands that they just wash over her completely. When reprimanding her, make your comments short and appropriate to her understanding. It also helps to put in some positives, such as 'You are normally so tidy which is why I'm annoyed at this mess.'

Could my child have a hearing problem? She never seems to listen when I speak to her.

This is a possibility. Partial hearing loss is more common than you probably think. Arrange for your family doctor to check her hearing. You'll probably find there is nothing wrong with her, although a proper hearing test will put your mind at rest. The difficulty is more likely to lie with her listening skills than with her hearing.

Your child will not focus on your words while engrossed in something else so get her full attention before explaining what you want.

5 Practical Principles

❶ **Say your child's name at the start of the sentence.**
Insert her name at the beginning of the sentence, then pause for a second, then say what you want. This catches her attention, making her ready to listen to what you have to say.

❷ **Make eye contact.**
Once you have attracted her attention, encourage her to look at you while you talk to her. Your child's listening improves when her attention is not distracted by something else. Eye contact facilitates better communication.

❸ **Ask her to repeat what you said.**
In a gentle, non-threatening voice, ask your child to repeat exactly what you just said to her. This strategy encourages her to pay more attention to your comments. However, be careful not to intimidate her.

❹ **Wait for a suitable moment before speaking.**
There is no point in, say, suddenly speaking to her while she is totally absorbed in watching a television programme. Either distract her first or wait until a suitable break arises.

❺ **Move closer to your child when you talk.**
She won't listen when you shout at her across a crowded room. The closer you are when you speak to her, the more likely your child is to listen accurately.

Emotional Problems

AGE 1–2 YEARS

Tantrums

Tantrums are common at this age, principally because your toddler expects the whole world to revolve around him. In this sense, he is very egocentric. His feelings are extremely intense; he does not like to wait, and he bursts with rage when his wishes are thwarted in any way.

Your Aim

To encourage your toddler to gain greater control over his temper, to express his anger verbally rather than physically and to cope calmly with disappointments.

AGE 2–3 YEARS

Thinking About Others

Now that your child interacts with others, he has to learn how to respond to their emotional needs – how to think about them, not just about himself. This shift away from being entirely self-focused and towards thinking about others creates emotional challenges as he gradually adapts to these new social demands.

Your Aim

To improve your child's social confidence so that he mixes positively with other children his own age.

AGE 3–4 YEARS

Self-confidence

Self-comparisons are common at this age. Increased social interactions provide your child with frequent opportunities to compare himself and his abilities to his peers'. If he perceives himself as less competent, then you may find his motivation drops and he begins to talk disparagingly about himself.

Your Aim

To promote your child's sense of self-worth and for him to accept himself positively, irrespective of how he compares to others.

Helpful Strategies

Never reward a tantrum by giving in to your toddler's demands. That would simply encourage him to have more tantrums in the future.

Stay calm. Repeat your earlier decision that he cannot get his own way. Be willing to say 'no', even in the face of his rage.

Look for the warning signs. Spot when your toddler is heading towards a tantrum, then try to distract him before he reaches explosion point.

Take time to talk to your toddler about his tantrums once he has calmed down. Although his understanding of right and wrong is starting to develop, he lacks control over his anger and frustration. So, it does not make sense to use punishments when he erupts in a temper tantrum. Instead, once it is over, sit with him, cuddle him and talk to him about trying harder to control his temper the next time.

Helpful Strategies

Boost his social confidence. Reassure him that the other children will like him if he behaves kindly towards them.

Try not to get angry when he bickers with other children. Instead, point out ways in which he could behave differently, so that fights can be avoided.

Give him plenty of opportunities to mix with his peers. This is important even though you and he might find this difficult at times.

Talk to him about his social experiences. Listen to the stories he tells about other children, offering advice as required.

Helpful Strategies

Remind him of his strengths. Point out all the reasons why you like being with him – for instance, he laughs a lot and he cares for others.

Be positive. Try to convince him that it doesn't really matter if his best friend can, say, run much faster or swim better than he can.

Support areas of desired improvement. For instance, if he is upset because other boys can run faster, practise running with him.

Highlight all his achievements. It is irrelevant how these compare to those of his peers or siblings.

AGE 4–5 YEARS

Social Rejection

Friendships assume greater importance now. Your child wants to be accepted by her peers, to be part of the group, and she experiences distress if this goal cannot be fulfilled. Any form of rejection – or simply not being included in their games – creates total misery for her.

Your Aim

To help your child to cope with the ups and downs of changing friendships.

AGE 5–6 YEARS

Fear of Failure

Achievements matter very much to a child at this age. For some, however, the fear of failure can be so daunting that they would rather not tackle a challenge at all than tackle it and fail. If your child is like this, you will notice that she avoids new experiences and is tearful when she fails to achieve her desired target.

Your Aim

To enable your child to have the courage and confidence to face new challenges, and to cope more effectively when success eludes her.

AGE 6–7 YEARS

Independence

Accumulated experience increases your child's desire to be independent. She wants to do more for herself, and to make her own judgements and choices. However, her ambitions probably outstrip her ability and she can end up in tears when she is unable to do what she had hoped.

Your Aim

To encourage her emotional need for independence, while protecting her from situations in which she is bound to fail.

AGE 7–8 YEARS

Self-identity

Your child is at the stage where her identity is forged. She develops her own views (not always yours), and she may start to have clear ideas about the clothes she wants to wear. At times she is very assertive, and determined – her psychological need for her own identity shows through.

Your Aim

To support your child in developing her individuality, even though at times this causes clashes between her and other members of your family.

Helpful Strategies

Encourage her to have more than one friend. This makes her less vulnerable to the whims of one particular child.

Pay close attention to her peer relationships. You will then be well placed to detect whenever there are disagreements or upsets between them.

Advise on conflict resolution. Suggest ways in which she and her friend could resolve their dispute after a fight.

Arrange for some of her friends to visit your house to play together. This helps strengthen your child's social connections with them.

Helpful Strategies

Explain that everybody experiences failure sometimes. Emphasize that in many instances success is built from the experience of failures.

Ensure that your child does not back away from challenges, despite her fear of failure. Encourage her to try anyway, even though she might not succeed.

Give examples of how you have learned from your failures. For instance, when you failed your driving test the first time, you learned to improve your weak points.

Cheer her up. Reassure her that she may well succeed at the next attempt, if she is upset by her lack of success.

Helpful Strategies

Show enthusiasm. Be delighted when your child announces to you that, for instance, she wants to try riding her bicycle by herself.

Do not hesitate to give advice. She may insist on managing on her own, but your suggestions teach her the benefits of listening to others.

Suggest a more realistic plan of action. This is especially important when you see your child about to embark on an activity that is obviously beyond her current abilities.

Offer new approaches. A fresh strategy can help if her ambition for greater independence is dampened through failure.

Helpful Strategies

Let her express her ideas. You may disagree, but at least give your child the chance to voice her opinions to you.

Give her support with choosing clothes. At times, let her pick the clothes she prefers. What she wears is a reflection of her identity.

Be prepared to guide her gently. Use subtlety, not confrontation, when you see her responding in ways of which you disapprove.

Explain to your child that she should respect the individuality of others. She should not make fun of them just because they are different from her.

moral and social development

5 moral and social development

- social awareness and play
- popularity
- social importance of body language
- friendship facts
- discouraging tale-telling
- making friends
- understanding shyness
- overcoming shyness
- dealing with bullying
- naughtiness
- confronting dishonesty
- discouraging unkindness
- being kind
- stopping aggression
- encouraging politeness
- moral and social problems

Social Awareness and Play

Your child is sociable by nature – although that might be hard to believe when you see your toddler screaming his head off because another child had the cheek to touch one of his toys! Nevertheless, he really does have an underlying emotional need to mix with others, to share with them and to be valued by them. However, his social awareness and his understanding of social rules develops gradually.

Social Play

Psychologists have identified four stages in the development of social play, and you will observe these different phases in your own child.

Stage 1: **Solitary Play**

This phase lasts from birth until around 15 months. Your infant has no interest in other children. He may not even notice them. If a child comes over to him, he probably stares blankly at him or starts crying with anxiety. Your infant generally loves attention from familiar adults.

Stage 2: **Onlooker Play**

In this phase, which lasts until about 2 years, your child shows greater interest in his peers although he still remains aloof. He might complain when you tell him he has to leave – which is surprising, as you thought he was not bothered about them at all. You'll probably also notice that your child starts to copy the play of other children he observes, but he continues generally to play alone.

From 2 years on children observe and copy other children though they may not play with them much.

Stage 3: **Associative Play**
Between 3 and 4 years, genuine social play emerges. Your child's increased social confidence and maturity mean that he understands the importance of social rules. When playing with his friends, he is more adept at sharing and turn-taking. However, arguments still remain common.

Stage 4: **Cooperative Play**
By the age of 4 or 5 years, your child finally plays in genuine cooperation with others his own age. He has come to realize that sharing toys, following an agreed set of rules and taking turns is the only way he and his friends can play together. Disputes are fewer, games become more complicated and last for longer, and he looks forward to meeting his friends the next time.

Learning to share is an important social skill which children begin to acquire between the ages of 2 and 3 and generally master by 5.

Social Development

3 months: Your baby has given his first smile. He loves being the centre of adult attention. He likes to keep you in sight, watching you carefully as you move around the room. He is easily distressed by unfamiliar faces.

1 year: His desire for interaction shows more clearly. He loves it when you play games with him, particularly those involving physical contact. Your infant looks closely into your eyes while you talk to him.

2 years: Although you find that your 2-year-old bickers a lot with his peers, he genuinely has fun in their company. He now learns that misbehaviour gets your attention.

3 years: Your child begins to recognize that other people have feelings, too, and that he can't always get his own way with his friends or his family. Specific friendships start to form.

4 years: He plays a lot more easily with his friends. You see the caring side of his nature, especially when a friend or sibling is distressed. His main topic of conversation is his pals and their games.

5 years: Peer group acceptance assumes great importance. Your child plays with the same children during school breaks, as they develop their own set of rules about play and friendships.

6 years: Your child's friendships are very variable. His best friend today might hold no interest for him a week from now. He likes people to follow social rules, and he becomes distressed when, for instance, another child misbehaves in class.

7 years: No longer the youngest pupil in the school, he begins to realize that he has some social responsibility for others. By now he probably has a couple of close friends, whom he has known for more than a year.

8 years: Social experience and stable friendships make your child more confident socially. He is not anxious about meeting new children or adults, and in fact may relish the opportunity. The majority of play activities are group-based.

Popularity

Friendships play a key role in your child's life. It is through peer relationships that she learns about her abilities, understands her strengths and weaknesses, and develops her social skills.

Every parent wants their child to be popular. A child who is popular:

- Feels good about herself.
- Is rarely lonely, because others want to be with her.
- Has a high level of self-confidence.
- Has a large circle of friends.
- Is in constant demand by her peers.
- Has lots of people willing to help.

Psychological research shows that popular children tend to share the same characteristics. First, they tend to be physically attractive. Second, they typically excel in at least one area – for instance, school exams, sport or music. Third, they generally have good social skills – they are good company and fun to be with.

Of course, you can't make your child an athlete if she is ungainly or a genius if she is an average pupil, nor can you change the way she looks – but you can help her develop social skills that make other children want to play with her.

Cooperation

Cooperation is a key social skill for popularity. It has three dimensions: practise with your child at home, so she can use them with her pals:

Children who can cooperate in play and win and lose graciously have an advantage when making friends.

5 Top Tips

❶ Show interest.
Take an interest in your child's friendships, talking to her regularly about her experiences with her pals whether at nursery, in the neighbourhood or at school. Try to assess her popularity.

❷ Discuss popular children.
Ask your child to tell you the popular children she knows and then ask her to explain why she thinks they are popular. This helps her identify the key features that lead to high social acceptance in her peer group.

Friendships can come and go amongst young children so it is ideal if your child has a wide circle of friends to play with.

❶ **Sharing.** Your child should be able to let others play with her toys without complaint. She should also be able to play with her friends' toys and return them when she has finished.

❷ **Turn-taking.** Most play involves one child taking a turn to do something before another. If your child barges in all the time, her popularity quickly plummets.

❸ **Following rules.** Children can't play games properly unless all the participants follow the same set of rules. Your child should recognize that the rules apply to her, too.

Communication

A child who can communicate effectively using spoken language is generally more popular than a child who communicates with actions alone. For instance, she does not win any friends by simply grabbing a toy from another child's hands – that sort of approach ends in tears, not friendships. Her relationships with her peers are more likely to be positive if she voices her feelings instead. For instance, she could say to her friend, 'I'd like to play with that toy. Could I play with it for a few minutes after you have finished with it?'

It is not easy for an impulsive young child to do this. She is so used to reacting first and thinking about the consequences later that the social technique of pausing, planning, speaking and then waiting is hard to master. Nevertheless, she can improve in this behaviour with your assistance. Encourage your child to speak before reacting, to make a request instead of snatching, and to voice her thoughts and feelings when appropriate.

Sensitivity

This is often a key characteristic of a popular child – she is the one who considers her friends' feelings and shows concern when one of them looks distressed, and also the one her peers can trust. Thinking of others, therefore, is another important social skill that will enhance her popularity.

That's why it is always helpful to ask your child about her friends' emotions. For instance, after a play session ask your child whether or not her friends enjoyed it. Then ask her how she makes that judgement – this encourages her to think more deeply about her peers' responses and emotions, which in turn increases her sensitivity.

❸ Provide popularity hints.
When trying to boost your child's popularity, offer one small suggestion at a time – for example, suggest that she looks more directly at other children when they talk to her. Aim for steady social progress, not large jumps.

❹ Encourage patience.
Your child might feel frustrated because she is not as popular as she would like to be among her age group. Explain to her that she should be patient and that friendships take time to form – they are not instantaneous.

❺ Give her realistic expectations.
Your child doesn't need to be the most popular child in her peer group – her goal should simply be to have more friends than she has now. She is more likely to succeed when her expectations are realistic.

Social Importance of Body Language

Research has demonstrated that in a friendship, a child typically expresses less than ten per cent of his emotions with words – most feelings are conveyed with body language. Language is used more to express facts. Your child talks far less than you think. While his non-verbal communication is in action all the time, he probably only uses words to communicate with his pals for less than 20 minutes in total every day.

First Impressions

Like it or not, first impressions count. People make judgements about others within the first few seconds of meeting them, based on their appearance, posture and general manner. This applies as much to children as to adults.

This means that the opinions that others form of your child are heavily influenced by his body language, because this is what they notice at first. Think about it for a moment. Do you feel heartened when meeting someone who has a scowl on their face? Do you feel enthusiastic when introduced to someone who keeps their arms firmly folded in front of them and does not make eye contact with you, but spends most of the time looking determinedly at the floor? Of course you don't, because that person's body language is negative and unwelcoming.

Teaching your child how to use body language positively helps him to create a good first impression, making others want to stay in his company long enough to get to know him better. This is not about social manipulation – rather, it is about using body language in order

Help your child to be aware that his body language will affect how other people perceive him – in this case as sulky and withdrawn.

5 Top Tips

❶ Develop his understanding.
Explain the significance of body language to your child. It probably hasn't occurred to him that his facial expression, posture and eye contact have any importance whatsoever.

❷ Increase his awareness.
To help your child improve his awareness of body language, get him to look at your facial expression and then ask him what he thinks you are feeling. Make this a game. Use a different facial expression each time.

to get a friendship off to a good start. Then, continued use of purposeful non-verbal communication helps to maintain established friendships.

Using Positive Body Language

Encourage your child to improve his body language in the following ways. Give him lots of practice, offering guidance and support where necessary:

- **Smiling facial expression.** A cheerful, broad smile is inviting. It suggests your child is fun-loving. That's far more attractive than a furrowed brow or even a completely neutral expression.
- **Head held upright.** If your child lets his head hang down – perhaps because he is shy or nervous – others will not find him approachable. He should try to hold his head upright, in a relaxed manner.
- **Eye contact.** Friends tend to look into each other's eyes for most of the time while talking to each other. Good eye contact is a sign of both strong social confidence and genuine interest in the other person.
- **Good posture.** Your child's confidence is partly communicated through his posture. Body language that signifies that he has high self-esteem includes straight (not slumped) shoulders, which are turned so that he is face-to-face with his friends.
- **Social distance.** Most communication between two friends occurs with around 45cm (18in) of distance between them. Closer than that creates a sense of discomfort and further than that suggests aloofness.
- **Hand movements.** When your child is socially anxious – for instance, when he meets other children for the first time – he probably rubs his fingers nervously. Try to encourage him to relax his hands when he is in social situations.
- **Arm positions.** A child who lets his arms hang loosely at his side appears more confident and welcoming than one who crosses his arms tightly in front of his chest, even though that might be his natural defensive reaction when entering a room.
- **Feedback.** Positive feedback during a conversation signifies genuine listening. Suggest to your child that he tries hard to nod in the right places and to wear a facial expression that matches the mood of the speaker's comments.
- **Body direction.** Turning away from another child in the middle of a conversation is inappropriate. It suggests boredom or rudeness. Advise him to face the other speaker until the discussion has clearly ended.

Encourage your child to hold his head up and make eye contact when he meets other people.

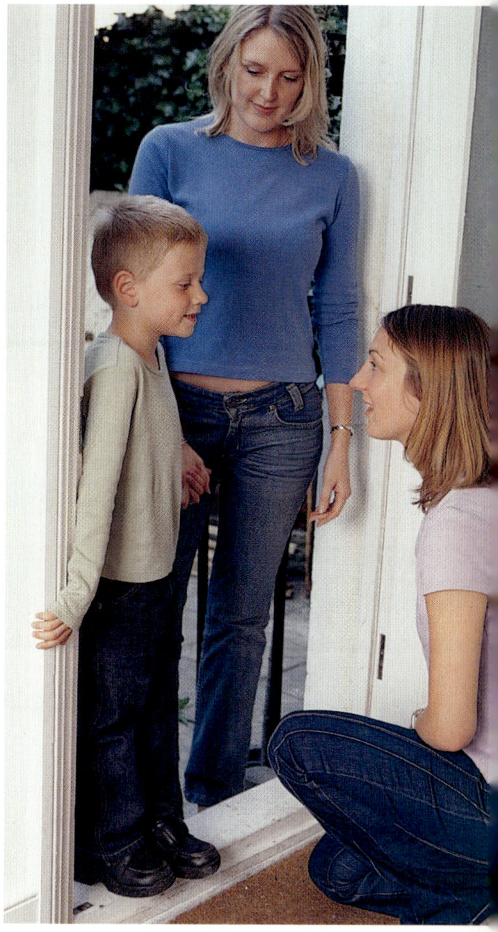

❸ Offer guidance.

Give your child basic suggestions to improve his body language, one at a time. For instance, he can practise improving eye contact for a few weeks before moving on to a different aspect.

❹ Praise success.

When you see your child use body language positively – perhaps when meeting a relative or friend – tell him how delighted you are that his body language was so confident. Point out the key features that were effective.

❺ Provide alternatives.

It is not enough for you to tell your child what is wrong with his body language – for instance, that his eye contact is weak. You also have to tell him what he should do – for instance, to look the other person in the eye.

Friendship Facts

Mixing with other children her own age is a very important part of your child's life. Here are some facts about children's friendships to give you a better understanding of the processes involved.

- Your child doesn't usually start to form identifiable friendships until she is 3 or 4 years old – before then, her friendships fluctuate.
- Some toys – for instance, a bat and ball – enhance social relationships because they develop cooperation between your child and her friends.
- Her first real friendship is most likely to be with someone of her own gender — they share an interest in common activities.
- The chances are that your child and her best friend are similar in age, personal characteristics, agility and understanding.
- Differences in friendliness are present at birth – some babies thrive on attention while others prefer interest from a few adults.
- Friendships in young children are practical – for example, they want to play with the same toy. Later on, friendships become based more on shared emotions.

Gender Friendships

Your child's interest in children of the opposite gender alters many times. Gender usually influences friendships as follows:

1–3 years: It is very unusual for a child in this age group to have developed a definite gender

Your child's friendships with the opposite gender are likely to fluctuate depending on her age.

5 Ways to improve friendships

❶ **Make sure your child has plenty of opportunity to play and mix with other children her own age.**

This can be a mixture of free play and adult-supervised activities.

❷ **Play a variety of games with her at home.**

This helps her develop tolerance and patience, as well as strengthening her social skills.

preference. In most instances, she plays comfortably with any of her peers who are pleasant towards her, whether boy or girl.

3–5 years: Gender plays a larger part in her choice of pals – most of her friends are the same gender. A girl often says she finds boys too noisy and rough, while a boy says that girls are not much fun.

5–7 years: Gender barriers seem to diminish now that she is at school. Girls and boys are expected to work together in their class groups – this temporarily increases friendships between them.

7–8 years: The earlier gender preferences re-emerge, especially in the playground. Girls generally play with girls and boys generally play with boys, especially when there are large numbers of both about.

As their imagination grows many children create imaginary friendships which can become very real to them.

Imaginary Friends

Research suggests that at least one-quarter of children under the age of 8 years have an imaginary friend at some stage. Although you might feel confused by this phenomenon, don't worry: your child knows her imaginary friend does not exist. She has fun with her fictitious pal even though she knows he or she is not real. Boys generally choose an imaginary friend who is more competent and talented, while a girl's selection is usually less able.

Although imaginary friends are part of normal child development, you should feel free to establish limits. For instance, you don't always have to leave an empty seat at the dinner table for her fantasy friend or give out an extra share of sweets. If you do give in to all her requests, you may discover that your child uses her imaginary pal in a manipulative way, perhaps to make herself the centre of attention. By all means ask your child to describe her 'friend' to you – she willingly gives you a description, though you may be surprised to find that her pal is actually an animal!

Be reassured: an imaginary friend doesn't mean your child is sad and lonely – most children who have an invisible pal also have plenty of real ones, too. If your child does have an imaginary friend, it is likely to appear for the first time when she is 3 or 4 years old and will probably disappear just as suddenly when she is around 8 or 9, if not before.

❸ Use positive reinforcement.

When you see your child play well with her friends, tell her how pleased you are that she is so caring towards her pals.

❹ Encourage her to play board games with her friends.

However, be ready to resolve any minor disputes that might arise before the game is over.

❺ Talk regularly to your child about her friendships.

Give her advice on how to resolve problems when any of her relationships become strained.

strategy: Discouraging Tale-telling

As your child grows, you unwittingly encourage two conflicting developmental trends. First, you want him to cope with his friends on his own, without having to run to you for help every time something goes wrong. Second, you want him to feel that he can turn to you whenever he needs help. It can be difficult to achieve a good balance between these two opposing dimensions.

If you don't get it right, one of the difficulties that emerges is that your child becomes a tell-tale – in other words, he constantly runs to you (or his teacher) in order to report another child's misbehaviour. Nobody, child or adult, likes a tell-tale and social rejection is bound to follow soon.

There are lots of reasons why a child likes to tell on others. Sometimes he simply believes firmly in rules. When he discovers another child has broken a particular rule and won't stop when told to, the only solution that occurs to him is to seek help from an adult. This is a positive sign of his moral awareness.

Questions and Answers

I often feel that my child tells tales to get attention. Could that be possible?

This could explain his behaviour. One way to get around this is to give him lots of attention when he doesn't tell tales (for example, take him on a special outing as a reward when he plays without complaining to you), and try to respond less when he does tell tales. Combining these strategies could be effective.

Should I just ignore my child when he tells me tales and send him away without listening?

It is probably best to listen because there may be something serious that he wants to tell you. If you ignore him completely he will start to feel that there is no point in sharing his worries with you at all. When you do listen, however, give a measured response so that he learns you don't always think it was necessary for him to come to you in the first place.

Of course, there are other children who tell tales on their friends in order to gain approval from their parent or teacher. A child motivated by this reason expects to receive reward or praise for his revelation, and is often surprised when reprimanded for his action. Telling tales on another child is also an effective way of gaining revenge, by using the adult to punish. No matter the underlying reason, however, tell-tales are never popular or trusted by their peers.

There is a fine balance between ensuring your child tells an adult when something is really wrong and discouraging tale-telling.

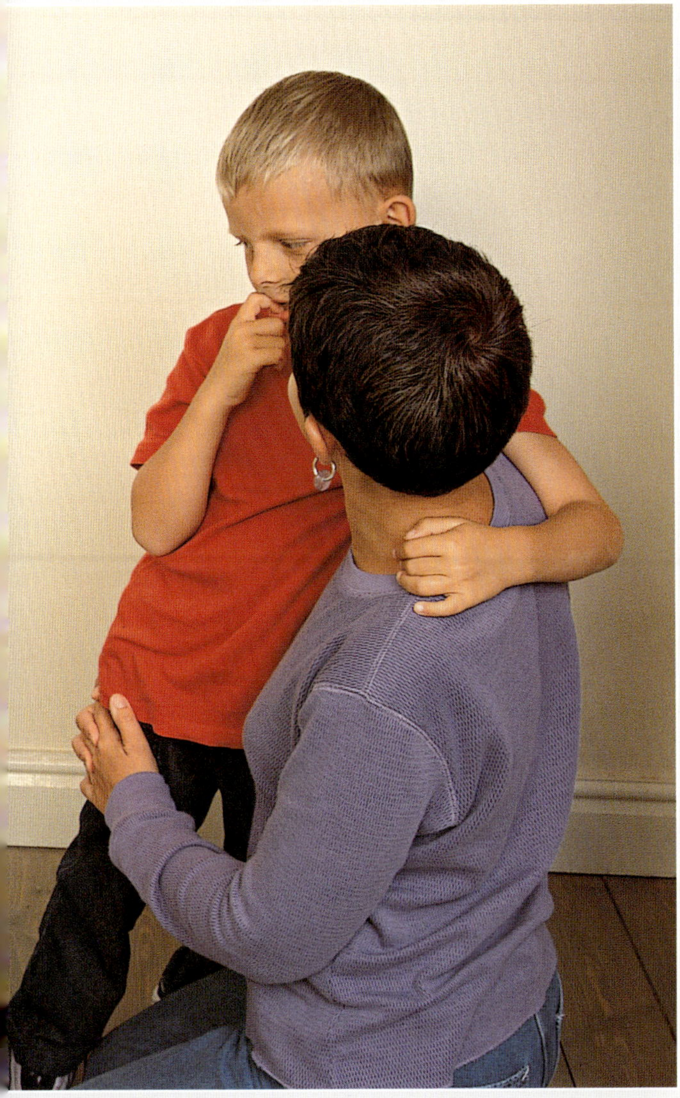

5 Practical Principles

❶ **Try to establish your child's motivation.** Repeated instances of reporting incidents of misbehaviour suggest that he is driven by an unsatisfied emotional need, perhaps for attention or maybe because he wants to curry favour with you. Once you establish the reason for his behaviour, you can begin to change it.

❷ **Don't tell him to keep his stories to himself.** While that strategy discourages his tell-tale behaviour, it also discourages him from telling you about those episodes that you do want to hear. Your aim is for your child to exercise discrimination over decisions about when to tell you something, not to cease altogether.

❸ **Explain the long-term effect of his behaviour.** Point out to your child that too many tales will result in the other children staying clear of him completely. They will not be able to trust him and they will be afraid to say or do anything in case he runs off to report them. Explain the practical effects of frequent tale-telling.

❹ **Suggest that he tries to resolve the problem first.** Instead of running to you the moment, say, one of his friends starts to mess about, he should speak to his friend first. Your child's confidence in coping on his own without turning to you for instant help increases the more he attempts to solve problems for himself.

❺ **Give advice rather than take action.** Your child expects you to react immediately he reveals a misdemeanour to you. Take a more reflective approach by suggesting a course of action for your child, one that does not involve you. This technique gradually discourages tale-telling.

strategy: Making Friends

It's heartbreaking when your child tearfully reveals to you that nobody wants to play with her. You know how important friends are to your child's happiness and development, and therefore you share in her distress. A child who is unpopular has a struggle maintaining her self-esteem – social rejection by her peer group dents her confidence badly.

Bear in mind that your child's claim of unpopularity could be exaggerated, based on only one or two specific incidents of social rejection. For instance, she could have had a fight with one of her friends in school, she feels miserable as a result and then announces to you rather dramatically that nobody at all wants to play with her. If she and her friend make up the very next day, she will forget that she ever made this earlier remark! Likewise, she might feel lonely and socially isolated if she does not receive an invitation to a classmate's party.

That's why you should always check out your child's claim that nobody wants to play with her, especially if you know that she normally has plenty of friends. Ask her to tell you the reasons for her sense of isolation. This type of discussion helps your child keep minor social disappointments in perspective.

Targeting New Friendships

Another possible technique for helping a socially isolated child improve her peer-group relationships is actively to encourage her to form new friendships. One of the difficulties with a child who is convinced nobody wants to play with her is that she feels disempowered, with no control over her social experiences. In other words, social rejection leads to passivity – so get her back in the driving seat using these strategies:

- Ask your child to identify two children with whom she would like to be friendly and who she thinks realistically could become pals with her. Let her take her time over this.

Giving your child the skills to socialize and make new friends may take time.

- Advise her to start to play with these children gradually – say, at the morning break for a couple of minutes. She should not hurry this process; it could take several weeks. Talk to her about this each day, giving more advice as necessary.
- When the friendships are partly established, arrange for her to invite her 'new pals' over to her house to play – and do what you can to ensure this proves to be a pleasant experience for all the children.

Questions and Answers

I understand why nobody wants to play with my child, because she is so horrible to them. What should I do?

The advantage is that you know where the problems lies: your child's social skills are weak. That's something you and your child can work at together in order to create improvement. Make this your goal. Identify the key social skills that are lacking in her social behaviour, then strengthen them. You should see progress within a matter of weeks.

I don't know what to do: every time my child plays with others her own age, they end up shutting her out. I have tried everything.

Consider enrolling your child in some type of leisure class, held locally. The nature of the class doesn't matter, as long as the theme interests your child. What matters is that she experiences social play within a highly structured, adult-supervised session. She will learn new social skills more easily in that context.

5 Practical Principles

1 Take your child's comments seriously.
If she does confide in you that nobody wants to play with her and you already suspect that she has social difficulties – maybe because she never seems to have other children to play with – listen to her views.

2 Tell her that you want to help.
Social isolation and rejection hurt badly during childhood. Your child feels vulnerable and afraid. Your supportive, caring comments are sure to raise her spirits straight away.

3 Discuss specific incidents.
Ask your child to describe in detail two or three recent incidents of social rejection that she has experienced. Make sure you get the whole story from start to finish; these accounts provide clues for future improvement.

4 Consider your child's contribution.
Of course, children do form cliques and they can be very exclusive of any child. However, consider whether or not your child's own behaviour might contribute to her social difficulties.

5 Offer her solutions.
For every problem there is a solution. For instance, she might try to behave more caringly towards her peers or improve her social skills. Offer some suggestions for change, then help her implement them.

Understanding Shyness

Psychologists cannot say for sure why one child is shy and another is not. Although there is a tendency for shy parents to have shy children, one child in a family may be shy while all her siblings are outgoing. Shyness is only a serious problem if it has a significant impact on your child's life – for instance, if she avoids other children at all costs. Mostly, shyness only causes temporary discomfort to a child (and her parents).

How shy your child is depends on the circumstances. Your child's shyness is influenced by numerous factors – the social context, her familiarity with those around her, her self-confidence at that particular moment, and the relationships she has with others. Shyness is a form of social embarrassment, as if she suddenly finds it all too much for her and wants to withdraw completely.

Shyness is also influenced by your child's age. The peak period of shyness is between 2 and 4 years, although there are plenty of shy children outside this particular age group. You may find that she's shy at one age and totally confident a year later, or vice versa.

Abuse

It can happen that a child avoids contact with adults because of an unpleasant experience, or perhaps even an instance of abuse. If you consider this is a possible explanation for any episode involving your child's unexplained shyness, talk to your family doctor in the first instance.

Shy children dislike being the focus of attention and usually respond by becoming withdrawn.

5 Reasons for shyness

❶ Lack of social confidence.
A shy child lacks belief in her ability to get on with others. She thinks that other children won't like her very much and so she totally clams up. Each time she experiences shyness, this reduces her confidence even further.

❷ Lack of social skills.
Your child may not know what to say to other children and adults when she meets them. 'Small talk' does not come naturally to every child – the sight of a roomful of strangers makes her mind go a blank and her mouth become dry.

Many children go through phases of shyness which they subsequently grow out of.

When You Embarrass Her

Parents have an amazing ability to embarrass their children! This is not a problem under the age of 5 years, but by the time she is 7 or 8 your child likes you to behave in a certain way when she is with her friends – and if you don't, she cringes with embarrassment. Previously, she used to think you were absolutely terrific, but now she's highly critical. It could be just the colour of your jumper that embarrasses her in front of her friends, or it might be when you give her a hug!

Don't take her reaction personally. Your child's social embarrassment at your behaviour is more to do with her need to establish her own identity, to prove to herself and her peers that she can make decisions for herself, and to demonstrate that her likes and dislikes don't always coincide with yours. This is actually a healthy step forward in her development.

The best way to deal with your child's claim that you embarrass her is to think about her comments and try to stop doing the things that make her wince. Try not to dismiss them out of hand. For instance, perhaps you could avoiding saying in front of her friends that it is time for her evening bath, and maybe you don't need to give her a hug and a kiss every time you collect her from her friend's house – if these actions make her face glow red, show some sensitivity and refrain.

If a small change in your behaviour would ease her embarrassment, then think seriously about doing this. The process by which you adapt your behaviour to her changing emotional needs is part of the meshing that goes on between parent and child during the school years.

❸ Dislike of attention.

A shy child typically hates being the centre of attention. She's just one of those people who likes to avoid the spotlight. The minute people give her their full attention, her face reddens and she is at a loss for words.

❹ Fear of social rejection.

Once a child has experienced rejection and exclusion by her peers, she starts to dread this happening again and only plays with a few good friends. When she is taken out of that comfort zone, her shyness operates in full.

❺ Low self-esteem.

When a child has a low opinion of herself, she expects others to take a similar view. No wonder, then, that she dreads big social events. She would much rather skulk in a corner away from everybody else.

strategy: Overcoming Shyness

The first stage in helping your shy child to beat his problem is to recognize the signs of shyness. This isn't always easy. Some indicators are obvious – such as a red face, poor eye contact and an inability to respond to direct questions. Others are more subtle – such as complaints of a sore tummy just before he is due to go to his friend's party, or lethargy during a social occasion when he is normally outgoing.

If you find that social events are consistently preceded by changes in your child's behaviour, then consider the possibility that they represent shyness and are his reaction to the impending social encounter. Talk to your child about this. He may be relieved to admit it.

First Steps

To help your child learn to overcome his shyness, it is important to acknowledge his difficulty. Let him know that you take his shyness seriously, and that you understand the pressure he feels when faced with the prospect of meeting new children and adults. He feels much better knowing that you are sympathetic to his emotional discomfort.

Give your child plenty of reassurance – he probably thinks that nothing can be done to help him. Reassure him that shyness can be changed. You could say that

A step towards tackling the physical side of shyness is to teach your child to make eye contact when talking.

you were shy as a child, too, and yet now you are very confident meeting new people. Your confidence in his potential progress makes him feel positive, too.

Bear in mind that your shy child's natural tendency is to avoid situations that make him feel shy, so he tells you that he doesn't want to go to the party or that he is no longer interested in continuing with the karate class. Discourage his avoidance tactics. He won't beat shyness by hiding.

Questions and Answers

How common is shyness in children?

It is very widespread. Surveys have found that almost four in five adults believe they had periods of shyness as children, and four in ten school-aged children describe themselves as shy when meeting new people. Remember that context matters, too: for instance, there is also some evidence that children are more likely to be shy in a highly competitive situation and less likely when they are expected to cooperate with each other.

My 7-year-old has suddenly become shy about having a bath in front of me. Is this normal?

You are confusing your child's natural desire for privacy with shyness. At this age, your child wants to set limits on who sees his body and he is perfectly entitled to do so. This is a sign of emotional maturity. It is important that you respect his need for privacy and don't make fun of him.

5 Practical Principles

❶ **Improve his social conversation.**
A common fear of the shy child is that he won't have anything to say to other children when he meets them, but you can teach your child some opening remarks. For instance, he can ask the other child's name, talk about his toys or discuss a television programme. Practise this with him.

❷ **Don't push too hard.**
The worst thing you can do is to push your child socially – and you may feel tempted literally to push him into a crowded room – as this only makes his shyness even more entrenched. Yes, he can be coaxed and supported out of his shyness, but he cannot be forced out of it.

❸ **Use his own 'territory'.**
The chances are that his shyness is less evident when he is on his familiar home ground. Use this to his advantage by inviting small groups of children (or even one child at a time) to your house to play. This boosts his social confidence for mixing in other settings.

❹ **Remind him of his strengths.**
It helps to remind your child of all the reasons why other children could like him. True, he probably shrugs off your comments as if they don't mean anything to him, but they will have a positive effect. Point out, for instance, that he is fun, with a good sense of humour.

❺ **Modify his body language.**
Concentrate on changing your child's body language so that the physical signs of shyness are less obvious. This includes having better eye contact, good posture so that he faces children he meets for the first time, and a smiling facial expression. Help him develop this at home until he appears more confident.

strategy: Dealing with Bullying

Bullying occurs when one person uses their power negatively to coerce and intimidate another. It is strange to think that such motives could be ascribed to a child, but the reality is that bullying occurs at virtually any age during childhood, even in the pre-school years. There is evidence that bullying occurs in nurseries, too. Stopping bullying can be very difficult as the wrong approach may simply make the situation worse for the victim.

You might consider that bullying is only to do with physical violence – such as hitting, punching, spitting and kicking – and this certainly is part of bullying in childhood. However, there are more subtle forms of bullying, including teasing the victim about his appearance, race or disability, tripping him up, whispering about him or even excluding him from a particular social group.

Never accept bullying as 'that's just children being children', whether your child is a victim or a bully. Bullying is never positive, it is always hurtful, and it reduces the victim's self-confidence and sense of well-being. Due to the damaging effects it can have in the long term, bullying should never be allowed to flourish.

Your Child the Bully

The possibility that your child might be a bully shakes you to the core, but if the evidence piles up – from reports by other parents or remarks by his class teacher – try to face this possibility. Children bully for many different reasons, ranging from insensitivity to a deep emotional need to assert themselves. Your child might not even realize the psychological damage he inflicts with his bullying.

- Confront your child calmly but firmly about the accusations. Explain the incidents that underlie your concerns and seek his views on the matter.
- Whatever his account, establish the definite rule that bullying of any sort is completely unacceptable, no matter how justified he might consider his actions to be.

Questions and Answers

What can my 8-year-old do to avoid being bullied in the playground?

A bully is more likely to pick on a solitary victim than on a child in a crowd. Advise your child never to be alone in the playground. He should always be with at least one other pupil and preferably a group. If he does not have a group of friends, suggest that he stands beside a group in the playground. This reduces his profile as a potential target. In addition, consider the strategies explained here (see Practical Principles, right).

My child has begged me not to speak to his teacher about bullying. Should I overrule him?

Yes, it is the only way. He is afraid that the bully will discover his disclosure and punish him even further, so you have to make sure this does not happen. Discuss anti-bullying proposals in detail with the teacher so that your child's name is not mentioned publicly – this contact with the teacher is essential. Tell your child of your strategy so that he trusts your judgement.

Bullying can cause children great misery and must be dealt with firmly and promptly.

- Make sure he understands that you will monitor his behaviour very closely in the future to check that his bullying has ceased.

With your support and encouragement, your child will gradually reduce his antisocial behaviour.

5 Practical Principles

❶ Do not dismiss your child's claim.
He has worked up a great deal of courage to tell you that he is bullied in school or among his peers locally and he deserves your sincerity, understanding and full attention. Even if the bullying appears trivial to you, it is highly significant to him.

❷ Discuss joint action.
Reassure your child that you will not take any unilateral action without keeping him informed – he may be terrified that you will speak to the bully's parents or teacher and that this will backfire, resulting in more abuse from the bully. Discuss everything with your child before reacting.

❸ Encourage a reduced response.
Of course it is difficult to ignore the taunts and hurts of a bully, yet the bully thrives on the victim's reaction. If the reaction is minimal, the chances are that the bully will leave that particular victim alone. That's why you should encourage your child to ignore the bully if this is at all possible.

❹ Never suggest retaliation.
A tit-for-tat response only escalates the tension further. The bully may actually delight in the counter-antagonism of the victim, prompting him to raise the bullying up a level. That cannot be good for your child – and in a physical fight, your child could easily be seriously injured by a stronger opponent.

❺ Speak to others.
Street bullying cannot be resolved without involving the bully's parents, and school bullying cannot be resolved without support from school staff. Explain to your child that you will raise your concerns very discreetly, in order to keep his name out of the process.

Naughtiness

Your child occasionally does things of which you disapprove – that goes without saying – but this does not automatically mean that all these actions are deliberately naughty. Think before you react because there could be other explanations. Be careful not to judge your child's action in the same way that you would judge a similar action by an adult. For your child's action to be regarded as genuinely 'immoral' in the real sense of the word, it has to meet several particular conditions.

Naughty behaviour occurs for a number of reasons including peer pressure and a desire for attention.

A naughty act must be:

- **Intended.** An accident isn't 'naughty'. However, if your child knowingly breaks a rule that you have set – for example, he deliberately takes an extra biscuit after you specifically told him not to – that places a different perspective on his behaviour.
- **Controllable.** You cannot justifiably accuse your child of naughtiness unless he has full control over her behaviour. So, for example, a young baby who knocks over the shampoo while you try to wash his hair isn't naughty because he does not have full control.
- **Insensitive.** When your child is naughty, he fully understands the potential consequences of his behaviour but makes a decision to ignore this in order to satisfy his own needs. It's this total insensitivity to others that makes behaviour immoral.

Stages Of Moral Development

0–2 years: An infant this age really doesn't grasp the difference between right and wrong. As far as he is concerned, 'right' means getting everything his own way and 'wrong' means other people stopping him. You can rarely accuse a child in this age group of being naughty.

2–3 years: Although he remains as stubborn as he was before, your growing child starts to listen to you. He understands the significance of rules, but still likes to suit himself. You'll find that he agrees wholeheartedly with your restrictions – and then promptly goes out and breaks them!

3–4 years: His moral development is more advanced now. However, he tends to base his moral opinions on the effect, not cause, of the action. This means, for instance, that he assumes that a child who deliberately breaks a plate is not as naughty as one who accidentally breaks dozens of them.

4–5 years: The moral balance shifts so that your child now places more weight on intentions instead of consequences. His line of defence when caught out is often 'I didn't mean to do it.' Understanding of right and wrong is well established.

5–6 years: A child of this age typically has such a strong sense of right and wrong that he becomes a self-appointed member of the morality police! That's why he spends a great deal of time telling off everybody at home when he thinks they have broken a rule. He likes to point out breaches of morality.

6–8 years: Your child recognizes that moral rules are not always rigid and that they often depend on circumstances. For instance, he might argue that a poor man is entitled to steal in order to feed his starving family. You may find that he challenges some of your rules.

So, think carefully before accusing your child of naughtiness. Consider the possibility that he simply did not realize what he was doing or that he was not aware of the rule he broke. The younger the child, the less likely it is that his behaviour has troubling moral implications.

Why Children Break Rules

Even when a child has full and mature moral development, he may still choose to break the rules. Lying, stealing and swearing are common during childhood, despite satisfactory moral awareness. There are several reasons for this:

- **Practical reasons.** For instance, your child steals a toy from his older brother's room because he wants to play with it, or maybe he tells a lie because he knows that telling the truth will land him in serious trouble. Much of childhood naughtiness is based on expediency.
- **Emotional considerations.** A child who feels unloved by his parents may steal money and food from them to compensate for his perceived lack of love – stealing is also his way of grabbing their attention. Your child might tell a lie in order to impress you: for example, if he wants you to think he is very sporty, he may say that he won the school race that afternoon even though he came last. He might also be naughty just for the thrill of it – misbehaviour can be more exciting than behaving well.
- **Social factors.** Peer pressure is often a dominating force when a child lies, steals or swears. The desire to win accolades from his friends tempts your child to misbehave in order to gain their admiration. If he mixes with other children who lie, swear and steal, then he'll soon start to behave like that, too. It's hard for a child to behave independently when he is with a group of pals.

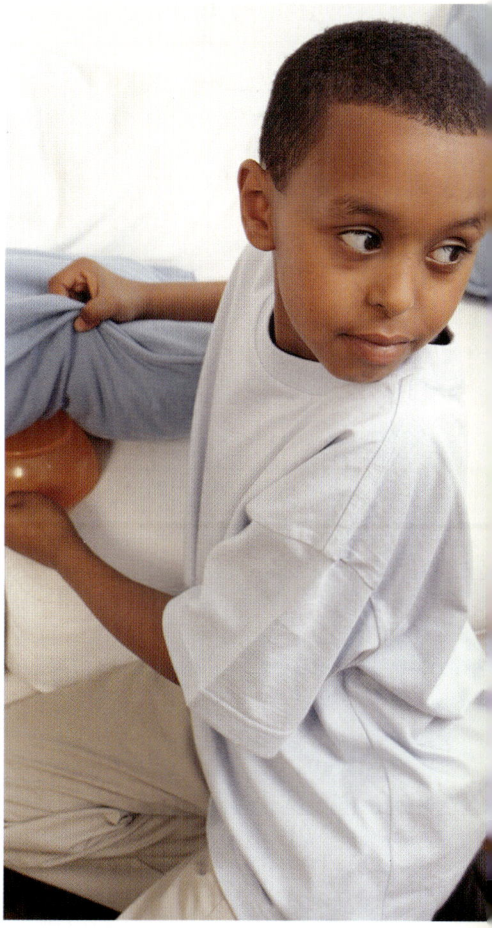

Children will often hide something that is broken or tell a lie to avoid getting into trouble.

strategy: Confronting Dishonesty

Most of the time your child is well-behaved, honest and polite. So it comes as a shock when you realize that he has told you a lie, or you discover that he has stolen something from his friend's school bag, or when you hear him utter a stream of foul language.

Lying

If you know that your child is lying to you about something, talk to him about it and consider using these strategies:

1. **Don't fly off the handle.** If your reaction is too extreme, your child will try twice as hard the next time to convince you that he is not lying, simply to avoid your anger. Disapprove, but don't lose your temper.
2. **Use reasonable punishments.** These should be appropriate to the severity of the lie. Excessive punishments mean your child is more likely to risk lying.
3. **Reassure your child that you love him.** He needs to know this is still the case even though you know he lied to you. He has to learn that you can be annoyed or disappointed with his behaviour, yet love him at the same time.
4. **Discuss what would have happened had he told the truth.** He will realize he would still have been in trouble, but that it would have been much better than having to deal with the consequences of lying.
5. **Urge him to tell the truth.** Explain that there will be times when he may find it too difficult to tell you something, but that you would always rather he told you the truth.

Questions and Answers

How can I explain why I told a 'white lie' about a present I didn't like?

Adults often tell 'white lies' to protect other people's feelings. However, a young child will find this confusing – especially since you have told him that lies are never acceptable. It's best to avoid this sort of lying in front of your child, at least until he is old enough to understand.

My child has been using swear words he picked up at school. What can I do?

This is probably the effect of his peer group. Explain your views on swearing and discourage him every time you hear him swear – this will have an effect eventually.

Stealing

You need to confront your child if you know or suspect he has been stealing. The following strategies may help:

1. **Talk about the effect of stealing on others.** Chat to your child about the impact his theft has on the victim. If stealing happens at school, consider talking the matter over with his class teacher.
2. **Do not accept stealing under any circumstances.** He may tell you that it was only a bit of fun, or that the other child has lots so he won't miss this one item. Explain that theft is never excusable.
3. **Suggest restitution where possible.** If it is practical, advise your child to return the stolen property to its original place. This does not need to be a public act – he can do it secretly.
4. **Offer him alternatives to theft.** For example, if you discover he stole money from his friend's jacket in order to buy toys, suggest that he could have asked you for extra pocket money instead.
5. **Use explanations and punishments.** The combination of appropriate punishment for theft, coupled with an explanation of why the theft was wrong, is the most effective way to discourage it.

A child may not understand the implications of stealing – explain why it is wrong and the effect it has on others.

Swearing

Your child is learning new words every day, so it is important to explain to him when his language is inappropriate. Keep the following strategies in mind:

1. **Never laugh at him.** It is often comical when a young child swears loudly, especially when he doesn't realize the significance of his words, but your laughter reinforces his swearing.
2. **Chat to him about the effect of swearing on others.** At first they might be amused but eventually other children will avoid playing with him. They will be uncomfortable with his language, too.
3. **Set a good example.** Think about your own use of language. In many instances, a young child swears because he hears these words used at home.
4. **Discourage peer influence as an excuse.** He may tell you that he only swears because all his friends talk like that. However, explain to your child that you want him to make his own choices, not simply follow his pals.
5. **Suggest different ways he can use language to express his frustration or anger.** There is nothing wrong in venting his feelings verbally, as long as he uses appropriate words.

5 Practical Principles

1. **Keep honesty high on your parenting agenda.** You should try to encourage honest behaviour from your child right from the start. Your focus on this encourages him to have a similar perspective, too.

2. **Keep things in perspective.** No matter how troubled you may be by an incident of lying, stealing or swearing from your child, it is not the end of the world. By all means, show your disapproval but don't be too extreme.

3. **Have discussions about morality.** Rather than waiting until your child breaks moral rules, talk about stealing, lying and swearing with him before such an incident occurs. Prevention through understanding can be very effective.

4. **Set reasonable expectations.** Remember that your child behaves according to his level of ability and understanding. You cannot expect him to make the same moral decisions that would be reached by an older child.

5. **Deal with the incident, then move on.** Once you have responded to an episode of naughty behaviour and have given guidelines for his future behaviour, look ahead instead of constantly referring to what happened previously.

strategy: Discouraging Unkindness

It is not in your child's nature to be unkind. On the contrary, his instinctive response is to be kind to others. So, if you witness an act of unkindness, you can be sure there is an underlying psychological explanation for his behaviour.

Questions and Answers

I know my 3-year-old doesn't mean to be thoughtless but he is. How can I make him think of others?

There is no easy answer to this because he is still at a self-centred stage of development. Nevertheless, gently point out to him when he acts without thinking of others. Stop him in his tracks and urge him to look at the impact of his behaviour on the other child. His sensitivity will increase steadily over the next couple of years.

Even if I cut the chocolate bar exactly in half, my two children complain that the other has a bigger share! Can this ever be resolved?

Your children's jealousy of each other is not about the amount of chocolate they receive from you and therefore they see differences where none actually exist. The only way to tackle this is by making each of them feel special to you, so that their need to compete with each other diminishes.

Cruelty

Perhaps your child is cruel to small animals because he doesn't appreciate that they experience pain and discomfort, or maybe he is cruel during an outburst of temper – his little brother just happens to be in the way when he expresses his rage physically. Some other incidents of cruelty by children are simple acts of revenge. Consider the following:

1. **Encourage your child to think of the victim.** Ask him to imagine how he would feel if he were on the receiving end of his cruelty. Developing compassion for the victim is very effective.
2. **Show your disapproval clearly.** Once your child grasps that his cruel behaviour does not please you, he is less likely to do the same again in the future.
3. **Reinforce his caring behaviour.** As well as displaying disapproval for acts of unkindness, praise him when he behaves kindly towards other people.

Thoughtlessness

So often, an apparently unkind act in childhood is really due to thoughtlessness, not to the deliberate intention to create upset. Bear in mind that your child is highly egocentric until he reaches the age of 2 or 3 years: until then he only sees the world from his own point of view and so, literally, does not stop to think about other people's feelings. From the age of 3 or 4 years onwards he becomes more sensitive to others, but he still tries to please himself most of the time. By the time he reaches school age his thoughtlessness has diminished significantly. Here are some strategies for encouraging thoughtful behaviour:

1. **Point out that other people have feelings, too.** Talk to your child until he understands that for most actions he makes, there is an emotional reaction from someone else.
2. **Try not to get angry with him.** His thoughtlessness does not stem from malice. It's a reflection of his immaturity, not of an underlying devious character.
3. **Give him tasks that involve cooperation.** Your child's thoughtlessness vanishes when he has to work with someone his own age.

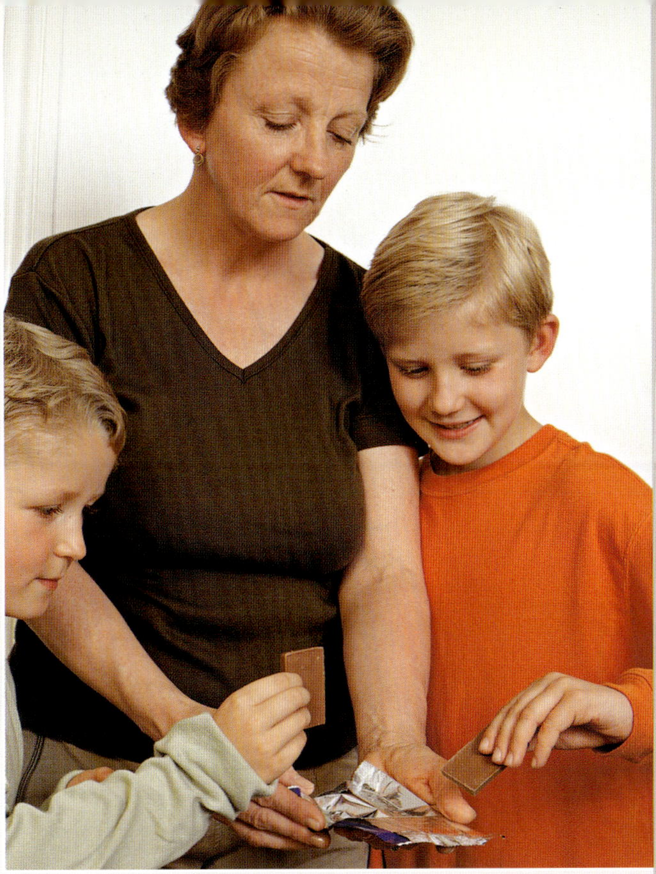

Avoid unnecessary triggers for jealousy by being scrupulously fair in the division of treats.

Jealousy

Isn't it amazing how quickly the green-eyed monster of jealousy surfaces? A moment ago your child was playing happily with his toys. Now that he has seen his friend's new truck, he begs you to buy him one – he wants what his friend has.

Jealousy is a very powerful emotion when it is aroused. Your child can be jealous of a material possession or of an achievement; he can be jealous of a friend, a sibling or a relative. Most children experience jealousy at times, so the following strategies may come in handy:

❶ **Don't make him feel guilty.** Remember that jealousy is a normal, universal emotion. There is nothing wrong in his feeling jealous as long as it doesn't overwhelm him.

❷ **Discuss times when you felt jealous of someone.** Let him see that you have similar feelings and that these emotions eventually subside. This will reassure him.

❸ **Encourage him to talk about his jealousy instead of acting on it.** Expressing jealousy verbally to you is better than acting on these feelings.

5 Practical Principles

❶ **Try to understand your child's motives.**
There is a reason why he behaves unkindly to others. Focus less on punishing him for his uncaring actions and more on the underlying reasons for his behaviour.

❷ **Show him ways to think about others.**
For instance, you can encourage him to plan ahead for his sister's birthday, so that he can make her a card or perhaps help choose her a present with you.

❸ **Boost your child's self-confidence.**
In many instances, a child's unkindness towards others stems from his own lack of self-esteem. Do what you can to make him feel good about himself.

❹ **Acknowledge jealousy when it arises.**
Instead of ignoring points of jealousy, make an empathic comment such as, "I can see that you are jealous but I'm pleased because you are trying so hard to overcome it."

❺ **Respond even to small acts of cruelty.**
He may think it is harmless, for example, to destroy insects (and you may think this, too). But discouraging even these minor acts helps him develop a more sensitive approach to others.

Being Kind

Many children are spontaneously kind and caring towards others, while some require encouragement to behave in this way. A kind child typically gets on better with his peer group and tends to be more popular.

Did you know that:

- **Your baby is instinctively caring.** If he hears a baby cry, he starts, too – and cries louder in response to a human cry than to a computer-generated one.
- **A toddler offers comfort to someone in distress.** When your 2-year-old sees another toddler in tears, he typically approaches that child and gives them a cuddle.
- **Bonding strengthens caring.** Studies have found that a baby with a strong emotional attachment to his parent will be more caring later on in childhood.

Helping to look after a pet can encourage your child to develop a more caring attitude.

Experimenting With Toys

In an experimental project, children were given two sets of toys to play with: either 'caring' toys (basketball and hand-held hoop that required cooperation, or medical play figures) or 'uncaring' toys (plastic guns or dolls that punched each other). After an hour or so playing with these toys, they were allowed to play freely with their friends. The children who had played with the 'uncaring' toys were more aggressive to their peers in the free-play session, while those who had played with the 'caring' toys were less confrontational, gentler and more cooperative.

5 Ways to encourage kindness

❶ Give him small tasks of responsibility.

Allocate a specific task to your child, such as putting videos back on the shelf or taking a biscuit to his brother. You could also make him responsible for feeding the family's goldfish or hamster.

❷ Praise any caring behaviour.

Wait for a spontaneous sign of caring from your child and then draw his attention to it. Your approval makes him more aware of that type of action, which he may have done instinctively without thinking about it.

Helping out in small ways and being praised for it will make a child feel the value of doing something for another person.

- **Caring actions encourage caring feelings.** A child who is required to help another person is more likely to develop a caring attitude to people in general.
- **Kindness is appropriate.** By the time he is 5 years old, your child is able to give appropriate practical help as well as emotional support to someone who is upset.

Dimensions of Caring

For your child to show genuine care and kindness towards other people, he needs three key emotional and social skills:

❶ **He has to be able to cooperate fully.** This involves working with another child, listening to that child's ideas and then reaching an agreed solution between them to which they can both contribute.

❷ **He has to be able to share.** This basic act of kindness involves your child having the confidence and trust to give something to someone else, without any guarantee that he will receive anything in return. Sharing is truly an act of kindness when looked at from this perspective.

❸ **He has to show empathy.** This is the ability to understand another person's feelings. While sympathy is also a sign of caring and understanding, empathy specifically requires emotional involvement in the other person's experiences.

For some children, these three qualities seem to develop naturally. For most, however, they develop slowly and steadily during the pre-school years. Be prepared to offer your child encouragement and guidance in order for him to acquire these caring skills.

Toys and Caring Behaviour

Common sense and everyday experience as a parent has probably taught you already that the toys your child plays with influence his behaviour towards others. You may have noticed that after your child plays a 'beat-'em-up' computer game, his play afterwards is more boisterous, perhaps even aggressive. This link between the effect of toys and behaviour is backed up by evidence from research and shows how important it is for your child to be able to distinguish between fantasy and his own behaviour.

❸ **Behave in a caring way yourself.**

Remember that your child models a great deal of his behaviour on you. If he sees you behave kindly towards others both at home and in the community, then he is more likely to start behaving in a caring way himself.

❹ **Encourage charity.**

Whatever amount of money he has – whether through regular weekly pocket money or presents for a special occasion – suggest that he gives a small amount to charity. Let him physically put the coins into the charity box.

❺ **Ask him to teach a friend or sibling to be caring.**

The act of explaining to someone else why he should be caring to others forces your child to clarify his own thoughts and strengthens his caring attitudes.

strategy: Stopping Aggression

It's one thing to be assertive – you probably encourage your child to have the confidence to stand up for himself when pressurized by others. Aggression is another thing – you are probably annoyed when you see him behave aggressively towards another person. However, your child may have difficulty knowing which is which! There is a fine line between assertiveness and aggression.

If your child is assertive, he:

- Expresses his feelings and ideas openly, without causing offence.
- Talks without making the listener feel intimidated.
- Achieves his goal without making someone else feel they have lost out.
- Uses positive body language to encourage a meaningful dialogue.
- Never uses physical violence in a discussion.

If your child is aggressive, he:

- Expresses his feelings and ideas in a way that harangues and offends.
- Talks in a way that makes the listener feel threatened and at risk.
- Achieves his goal at the clear expense of someone else's interests.
- Uses negative body language to discourage any meaningful dialogue.
- Is willing to use violence during a discussion.

Developing Your Child's Assertiveness

- **Encourage him to have confidence in his own opinions.** An assertive child thinks clearly, verbalizes his ideas in a way that the listener understands and has belief in the worth of his views. That's why it is important to encourage your child to talk when he is at home and to say what he thinks, and to let him see that you value his opinions even if you disagree with him at times.
- **Encourage him to listen with understanding when someone gives him their views.** He has to demonstrate that he is listening, through eye contact and other non-verbal feedback.
- **Develop his sensitivity to the other person's feelings.** Your child should not simply ride rough-shod over others in order to achieve his own aims.

Children need to learn how to manage feelings of aggression so they are able to be physical without losing control.

- **Practise his summarizing skills.** This allows him to précis both sides of an argument and then repeat his own view once more.

Assertive children don't always get their own way, but then neither do aggressive children. With your support, your child will learn from experience the most effective style of interaction when sharing conflicting views with his peers. This is a lot better than simply lashing out at the other child when they are in disagreement.

Questions and Answers

I find that when I shout at my child for hitting or kicking he stops instantly. Is there anything wrong with my doing that?

If it works effectively with your child, then that is obviously one way to discourage his aggression. Many children, though, are more responsive to a strong, firm parental voice than to an aggressive one. Ultimately, it comes down to knowing your own child and using a fair and reasonable method that will work with him.

How can I get rid of my child's aggressive streak? He starts slapping and hitting the minute he loses his temper.

You won't be able to remove his aggression altogether as it is part of his personality. Instead, your aim should be to help him gain control over this powerful innate feeling and redirect it in a less antisocial way. Use the strategies mentioned (see Practical Principles, right). Remember that when it is controlled and used positively, aggression can help your child achieve a goal – for instance, to win a race or persevere at a challenging task until he has completed it.

5 Practical Principles

1 Deal firmly but non-physically with your child.
There is plenty of research evidence to confirm that while smacking an aggressive child may have a short-term effect, in the long term it increases his aggression.

2 Use clear, distinctive punishments.
Any punishments given in response to your child's aggression should be fair, reasonable, and have a clear start and finish. Try to give the punishment as close in time to the actual incident as possible.

3 Point out the implications of your child's aggression to him.
For example, explain to him that hitting the other child made her cry and that she will be afraid to play with him in the future. Spell out the consequences that his aggression has for her.

4 Give your child frequent reminders.
There is no harm in giving your child regular warnings about his aggression, especially before he starts to play with his friend or when you see his temper rising with his little sister.

5 Be aware of possible influences.
Monitor his television viewing to ensure that he does not watch aggressive programmes that are aimed at a late-night adult audience. His aggression may be influenced by what he sees on television.

strategy: Encouraging Politeness

Good manners are not simply about social niceties and etiquette – the reality is that children with good manners are more popular and easier to get on with. Nobody likes to spend time with a child who makes constant rude noises, barges to the front of the queue, interrupts mid-conversation or demonstrates obvious signs of impatience with another person.

A display of bad manners creates social distance between a child and his peers. It is true that a group of children will burst out laughing when one of them makes an unexpected rude noise or says something cheeky to an adult, but the joke soon wears thin.

Few children acquire good manners naturally – in most instances, manners have to be learned through advice and social experience. There is nothing like his peers' complaints and protests when he rudely breaks into the head of queue to make your child think again about his observance of social rules. The same applies when he eats in a disgusting way with his classmates at lunchtime. Peer reaction is an effective teacher.

You also have to provide guidance. At times your child might not immediately grasp the value of a particular social rule, so try to explain its underlying purpose – for example, say 'If you don't interrupt me while I speak, I won't interrupt you when you speak.'

Expectations of Manners

Don't expect too much of your child. Manners typically develop at the following pace:

Teaching and reinforcing good manners so they become automatic will give your child a social head start.

- **2–3 years:** Your child likes to do what he wants but he is becoming aware of manners. He begins to remember the social rules you have told him, although he may not observe them.
- **3–4 years:** He is conscious of politeness because he likes to gain adult approval. He revels in praise for his good manners and may over-exaggerate them.
- **4–6 years:** Because your child mixes more with others, particularly at school, he realizes the social importance of manners and consequently makes more of an effort to be polite.
- **6–8 years:** At this period your child may think it is exciting to be rude deliberately – his friends egg him on. Reinforce good manners in these instances.

Questions and Answers

I am fighting a losing battle, because every time my 4-year-old makes a rude noise at mealtimes my older children burst out laughing, which only encourages him. What can I do?

The targets for change should be all your children except your 4-year-old. It is your older children who are obstructing any progress with his manners by positively reinforcing his rudeness with their laughter. Speak to them in confidence, explaining the negative effect they have on their younger brother. Once they stop rewarding his bad manners with laughter, his politeness will steadily increase.

What can I do to make my 8-year-old more patient? He explodes with anyone in our family, either child or adult.

Explore the possible causes. For instance, he could be worrying about something (like school or friends) that reduces his tolerance for others, or he could be trying to develop his own identity and personal space. It's time for you to have a long and private chat with your child about his impatience with his family. Listen to what he has to say and offer advice on other ways to respond.

5 Practical Principles

❶ Rudeness: point this out to him.
Your child might not be aware that his behaviour was impolite, and if he is aware, your reminder is a good prompt for encouraging better manners the next time. Tell him how he should have behaved.

❷ Impatience: encourage him to try harder to control his frustrations.
It helps to explain that the other child was trying his best and that expressing his impatience to a struggling friend only makes that child feel under even more pressure.

❸ Selfishness: let him know you are disappointed with his lack of sensitivity.
Discuss with your child what would have happened had he shown more thought for others instead of putting himself and his needs first. This lets him see the alternative possibilities.

❹ Intrusiveness: ask your child to wait until you have finished before stating his point of view.
His impulsive instincts drive him to voice his ideas the moment they arise, but he can gain control over this. With some effort, every child can learn to manage his tendency to interrupt.

❺ Sneering: explain that this damages the other child's self-confidence.
Suggest that before he makes disparaging comments, he should think how he would feel to be on the receiving end of such an attitude.

Moral and Social Problems

AGE 1–2 YEARS

Social Awareness

Your infant is only just becoming aware of right or wrong at this stage – she responds to her immediate impulses without any concern for either her own safety or the effect this has on anyone else. She generally likes attention from other children and adults she knows well, but often clings tightly to you in unfamiliar social situations. When mixing with other children her own age, she may refuse to share her toys with them.

Your Aim

To encourage your toddler to be more relaxed around other children and for her to begin to follow rules more appropriately.

AGE 2–3 YEARS

Disputes

Your child now understands the significance of the rules and limits you set, yet in many instances she still decides to do what she wants – and when you stop her, her fury erupts. She expects to get her own way and genuinely cannot understand when her wishes are blocked.

Your Aim

To establish rules of behaviour at home for your child and to provide a variety of social opportunities for her throughout the week.

AGE 3–4 YEARS

Naughtiness

Because your child judges the morality of her behaviour in terms of its consequences, not its underlying intention, you may find yourself reprimanding her for something that she regards as minor and trivial. For instance, she doesn't understand why you are so annoyed that she deliberately broke that small ornament – as far as she is concerned, it was only little! Many children of this age can be very antisocial at times, even with their pals.

Your Aim

To develop your child's moral understanding so that she grasps why some actions are considered wrong, and to improve her ability to resolve any conflicts she may have with her peers.

Helpful Strategies

Take her along to parent-and-toddler groups. You will be there with her anyway, so you can sort out any social difficulties as they arise.

Encourage her to think about other people. Even at this age she can begin to guess how her older siblings will react if she touches their possessions.

Show disapproval when she misbehaves. She begins to understand the difference between right and wrong, and she often knows when she is being naughty.

Respond to her communications. Despite her limited speech, react when you see she is upset about something. This enhances her social sensitivity and sets her a good example.

Helpful Strategies

Do not give in to her temper. Now that she understands what rules mean, she just doesn't like the fact they apply to her personally.

Begin to use rewards and punishments for managing her behaviour. Always explain to her the specific reason for using these.

Do your best to calm her when she loses her temper. She needs you to help her regain control.

Give your child small responsibilities that involve caring for others. For instance, she can hand the biscuit tin to her older sister. Praise her when she does these tasks appropriately.

Helpful Strategies

Explain to her why you are unhappy with her innappropriate behaviour. Discuss the consequences that her actions have for others.

Set clear moral rules. Ambiguity is unhelpful. For example, make sure she understands that stealing and lying are totally unacceptable.

Teach her about compromise and negotiation. This will help her sort out conflicts when playing with friends and she will start to understand even at this age.

Avoid physical punishment no matter how difficult she is at times. Smacking will simply make her try harder to conceal her misdemeanours from you in the future.

AGE 4–5 YEARS

Fear of Discovery

Your child can be very determined to conceal his actions, especially when he realizes that you are unhappy with his behaviour. His fear of discovery in this situation is extremely strong so do not be surprised to be faced with a denial even though you caught him mid-action.

Your Aim

To help your child begin to make basic moral judgements himself, without you having to tell him right from wrong every time.

AGE 5–6 YEARS

Peer Pressure

Your child spends much of his typical weekday with his peers and consequently responds to their ideas and beliefs. You may find that he favours their moral values, resulting in conflicts over his behaviour. Your child will do almost anything to be accepted by others his own age.

Your Aim

To encourage him to make moral judgements based on your consistent values, not simply on the views of his peer group at the time.

AGE 6–7 YEARS

Challenging Rules

The confidence that comes from attending school and making progress there often leads a child of this age into believing that he can challenge moral rules. For instance, he might confide in you that he believes stealing from a shop is acceptable because it doesn't hurt anyone.

Your Aim

To encourage your child's independent thinking, while also explaining to him that basic moral values should not be changed according to his needs and desires.

AGE 7–8 YEARS

Antisocial Behaviour

You may find that your child and his friends think it is 'cool' to misbehave deliberately, such as stealing from a local shop, and that it is exciting to do something naughty and then run off. Antisocial behaviour can seem attractive because it is adventurous and non-conformist.

Your Aim

To help your child to mature emotionally and psychologically, without running into problems created by peer group pressures.

Helpful Strategies

Encourage him to mix with others. As well as learning from you, he learns from his peers about morality and rules.

Discourage any form of lying. Explain to your child that it is better to tell the truth the first time than it is to lie in order to avoid facing a reprimand.

Talk to your child about incidents that have moral dimensions. For instance, discuss the time when his friend took a toy from him without asking.

Have higher expectations of his social skills. Let him know that you think he should be able to play with his friends harmoniously.

Helpful Strategies

Talk to your child about his friends, their ideas and their personalities. It is important for you to know the children he mixes with regularly.

Encourage moral understanding. Make sure you offer good explanations to your child. Rewards and punishments alone won't have as much effect as they did when he was younger.

Remind him that he should make up his own mind. Never be satisfied with the explanation that he did something wrong 'because the others told me to'.

React quickly and reasonably. For instance, if you see items in his schoolbag that you do not recognize and are sure do not belong to him.

Helpful Strategies

Discuss the significance of moral rules with your child. Ask him to imagine how society would be if nobody followed rules and everybody did exactly what they wanted.

Give your child space to express his moral ideas. Do this even if you disagree with him, and express your opinion. This is an important dialogue.

Encourage your child to see the wider moral implications of his behaviour. He should consider not just himself but his friends and family, too.

Chat about artificial moral dilemmas. For example, discuss what a poor, hungry man should do if he sees a rich person drop some money in the street.

Helpful Strategies

Deal with any incident of stealing or lying very firmly. Do not show sympathy towards his explanation that it was 'just a bit of fun'.

Explain that you talk to his teacher regularly. He knows this means you will always hear about whatever happens to him in school, good or bad.

Respond immediately to any episodes of bullying – it should never be tolerated. You need to react whether he appears to be the victim or the bully.

Try to ensure that he invites his friends to your house occasionally. This is a good way to assess the suitability of his current peer group.

Index

acknowledgments

Photography: Peter Pugh-Cook, except for the following:
Octopus Publishing Group Limited/Steve Gorton
126/William Reavell 71
Photodisc 13

Executive Editor **Jane McIntosh**
Editor **Rachel Lawrence**
Executive Art Editor **Joanna MacGregor**
Designer **Ginny Zeal**
Picture Research **Jennifer Veall**
Production **Manjit Sihra**